EVERYTHING BY PRAYER

Everything by Prayer

Armin Gesswein's Keys
to Spirit-Filled Living

Fred A. Hartley III

CHRISTIAN PUBLICATIONS, INC.
CAMP HILL, PENNSYLVANIA

CHRISTIAN PUBLICATIONS, INC.

3825 Hartzdale Drive, Camp Hill, PA 17011
www.christianpublications.com

Faithful, biblical publishing since 1883

Everything by Prayer
ISBN: 0-87509-973-4
© 2003 by Fred Hartley
All rights reserved
Printed in the United States of America

03   04   05   06   07   5   4   3   2   1

*Note: Italicized words in Scripture quotations
are the emphasis of the author.*

Dedication

To pastors and intercessors with a passion to see their churches become a "house of prayer for all nations."

Contents

Foreword

In 1970, as the pastor of a growing congregation in Kent, Ohio, I found myself in the midst of a city in revolution. People were being killed and wounded by National Guard bullets. It was a moment of desperation when clearly the *only* thing we could do was *pray*.

During six intensive weeks of intercession, I was handed an article on prayer by an author I'd never heard of: Armin Gesswein. To my joy, he described precisely my vision for the believers in Kent: "The world has yet to see," he wrote, "what God can do in and with and through a church wholly devoted to Him in prayer." I was determined we would try. As a result, the Spirit birthed a burden for prayer and revival that has motivated my life ever since. Over the ensuing years, I labored, in many contexts, toward the fulfillment of Armin's challenge.

Then, almost thirty years to the day after I read his article, I found myself in a prayer meeting *with* Armin Gesswein, in Los Angeles, along with nearly a thousand other pastors. At one point they called me to the front to lay hands on me and pray for my ministry. To my sheer delight, Rev. Gesswein offered the prayer. With other leaders gathered round, this "apostle of prayer" appealed to heaven to take my message of Christ-centered revival to the nations. For me it was like coming full circle.

Over the next fifteen years, Armin continued to mentor me—in his writings and letters, by his prayers over me, and by hours of rich, private conversations. He discipled hundreds of other leaders the same way. Now *you* can join our happy band, thanks to this skillful compilation of stories and secrets by Fred Hartley, another Gesswein protégé.

The director of the Colleges of Prayer, Fred provides a host of timely treasures in one unique volume. First, he feeds us plenty of

"Arminisms"—pithy principles drawn from the crucible lifestyle of a God-seeker. He introduces us to some of Armin's insights on prayer's relationship to evangelism, church life, spiritual growth and Spirit-filled ministry, along with potent instructions on how to pray like Jesus. You can't walk away from this book without being sold on one of the greatest of all Arminisms: "Prayer must be *frontal*, not *peripheral*."

Fred also favors us with some autobiographical tidbits. Woven throughout, they show the transforming effect Armin's mentoring could have on any teachable Christian leader. In fact, as I read the chapters I almost felt like Armin was sitting beside me again, doing what he did so well—walking me into the depths of prayer, one step at a time. That's why I'm grateful that Fred put discussion questions after each chapter, to encourage us to form mentoring groups and wrestle with these issues together.

But above all, the lasting impact of *Everything by Prayer* for me—in fact, the greatest blessing I ever derived from Armin's life and teachings—is the Christology. It's Armin's vision of who Christ really is. As he says:

Christ died the way he lived—praying.

When Jesus built the Church, He built a prayer meeting.

When Christ gives revival, He gives Himself.

Christ alone is the completely *vertical* Person. [That's my favorite!]

Incidentally, the phrase "everything-by-prayer" should remind us to read this book by prayer—in other words, to read it *vertically*. Armin Gesswein would have it no other way.

David Bryant
President of Concerts of Prayer International
Chairman, America's National Prayer Committee

Introduction

My Mentor, My Friend

I was sitting on the front row of Armin Gesswein's memorial service, squeezed like a sardine between twelve other men selected to pay him public tribute. I silently reflected, *How can I possibly express the impact this man has had on my life in three skimpy minutes? You can barely poach an egg in three minutes!*

Forty-five years my elder, he could have been my grandfather. And in a sense he was—my spiritual grandfather. I loved Armin. I loved him for the invaluable deposit he made in my life. Like a dad, he poured his life into me; like a coach, he instructed me; like a friend, he walked with me; like a teammate, he challenged me; like a mentor, he believed in me. And like a grandfather, in his eyes I could do no wrong.

Armin and I have put a lot of miles on our tires. We have traveled together for over thirty weeks from coast to coast and twice overseas. We have facilitated prayer summits and prayer conferences on college campuses, at retreat centers and in local churches. I have on file over 200 handwritten letters and 400 prayer letters. I have heard him preach-teach hundreds of sermons and have read everything he ever published, including his previously unpublished graduate school thesis.

While slicing and dicing my brief memorial service tribute, I quickly became absorbed in the stories from men with whose reputations I was well familiar: Dr. Ray Ortland, previous pastor of Lake Avenue Presbyterian Church; Dr. Bob Bowman, president of Far East Broadcasting Company;

1

Sherwood Wirt, editor emeritus of *Decision* magazine; Dr. Ted Engstrom, past president of World Vision; and Harold Sala, president of Guidelines. I felt like I was sitting in the batter's box awaiting my turn in a baseball lineup with Reggie Jackson, Mickey Mantle, Willie Mays and Babe Ruth!

They referred to Armin as "the most focused man I have ever met," "my prayer partner," "one of the greatest influences in our generation." As I listened to each of these men eulogize Armin, I was gripped by the realization that I had been just one of many whose lives had been profoundly shaped by this generous mentor. He had invested in each of us as if there were only one of us.

Of all the stories told that day, perhaps the most gripping was the story of the prayer meeting that is said to have launched Billy Graham's world-impacting evangelistic ministry. I caught myself sitting with my mouth literally hanging open as I listened for the first time to the following account.

It was 3 o'clock in the morning on Wednesday, July 13, 1949. Between forty and fifty young men were gathered in the Rainbow Room of the Westminster Hotel in Winona Lake, Indiana. They had been there for five hours—praying. Evangelist Armin Gesswein of Southern California, who had been invited to conduct the prayer sessions, exhorted Billy, "If you are going to have prayer as part of your crusade, it has to be frontal, not peripheral." That is exactly how an all-night prayer meeting happened to be called in the midst of a busy week-long Youth for Christ convention. The men had been alternating prayers with praise, verses of Scripture and requests for more prayer.

Things were beginning to warm up. Hearts were poured out before God. The tide was running high. Gesswein stood to his feet. "You know," he said, "our brother Billy Graham is coming out to Los Angeles for a crusade this fall. Why don't we just gather around this man and lay our hands on him and really pray for him? Let's ask God for a fresh touch to anoint him for this work."

When it was over and the men were still kneeling, Billy Graham opened his Bible to Joel 3:13 and with deep conviction read aloud the words, "Put in your sickle, for the harvest is ripe: Come, get you down: for the press is full, and the vats overflow." Prayer went on in the Rainbow Room for another hour before the men retired.[1]

Dr. Robert Cook, past president of King's College in New York, vividly remembers that night. "We prayed in faith and felt that we got through to God."

Another eyewitness reported,

At once we knelt around him. Wave after wave of prayer flooded our hearts. It seemed we had a hotline to heaven. Intercessory prayers stormed the gates of heaven for Billy Graham and for revival to come to Los Angeles. And we somehow knew the answer was on the way. Still kneeling there and looking like a young prophet, Billy said, "I believe if we will put in the sickle we will reap an unprecedented harvest of souls." When it all happened a few months later in Los Angeles, the reporters were there and the harvest became front-page news. But the newspapers did not report that night of prayer in the Rainbow Room.

Dr. Ted Engstrom reflected, "No one who was at that prayer meeting in Winona Lake in 1949 could possibly have forgotten it. It was one of the greatest nights that those of us present could ever remember. One aspect of it was the complete unanimity of spirit. Practically all of the men present found places of significant leadership in evangelism in the days following."

I thought to myself as I listened attentively, *How could I have known Armin for so long and yet he never told me about this?* I quickly concluded, *Well, that's just like Armin, a master of understatement, not to elevate himself nor draw attention to his own accomplishments.*

I learned that day that when the Los Angeles Crusade began in 1949, Billy Graham preached to the masses of Hollywood celebrities crowded into the preaching tent, and Armin Gesswein was leading a prayer service in a separate "prayer tent" where up to 1,000 lesser-known people quietly gathered to cry out to God. They were asking God to rend the heavens and come down, for God to pour out His Holy Spirit, to anoint Billy Graham, for people to be convicted of their sin and to dramatically repent and be converted. Young Graham himself consistently came into the tent for prayer prior to preaching. It has been said that without the effectiveness of the intercession from the prayer tent rising before God's throne, there may well have not been life-transforming power falling from God's throne in the preaching tent.

Concerning Armin's ministry, Billy commented, "I will never forget how he challenged people all over Southern California to pray for our meetings way back in 1949. And I believe that from that day until he recently went home to heaven, this great prayer warrior interceded for me and my ministry and encouraged others to do likewise."

On November 7, 1983, Billy Graham stood on the corner of Washington and Hill Streets in Los Angeles at the exact spot of his prior crusade to receive an award from Mayor Bradley as a marker was erected to commemorate the historic significance of what took place in 1949. However, the launching of the Billy Graham Evangelistic Association may not have come from the preaching tent at the Los Angeles Crusade in 1949 as many have assumed, but from the pre-Los Angeles Crusade prayer meeting in Winona Lake and the Los Angeles prayer tent. God keeps the books and when they are opened from the other side of eternity, we may be surprised to learn the invisible interplay between the private little prayer meetings and the great big public results.

Still sitting on the front row at the memorial service awaiting my turn to speak, I learned that in addition to Billy Graham, Armin's influence extended to a veritable "Who's Who" of Christian leaders, including Bill Bright, founder of Campus Crusade; Chuck Smith, senior pastor of Calvary Chapel; Richard Halverson, chaplain of the U.S. Senate; David Bryant, founder of Concerts of Prayer International; Charles Fuller, founder of Fuller Theological Seminary; and the prolific author A.W. Tozer.

Armin's passion was for revival in the church, resulting in effective evangelism in the world. He lived with a heavy burden that the modern prayer movement not be a mile wide and an inch deep. He tediously, meticulously taught prayer principles which stuck in our minds and radically influenced our lives.

As I stared eyeball-to-eyeball into the life-sized, full-color portrait of Armin which stood shoulder high, smack in front of the pulpit from which I was about to speak, it seemed to brim over with his infectious smile. That photo stimulated a flash flood of significant moments from the treasure chest of my memory bank. It was almost as if I could hear his winsome voice speaking those golden nuggets which over the twenty years of our friendship have been burned into my mind. His inner circle of friends affectionately calls them "Arminisms":

"If the Holy Spirit doesn't do it, there's nothing to it."

"God always does His new things in the same old way."

"The main things of Scripture are the plain things; and
the plain things are the main things."

"God wants us to put all of our begs in one ask it."

> ## "If we do what God tells us to do, He will do what He says He will do."
> ### —Armin Gesswein

These nuggets and a host of others will be generously
sprinkled throughout the following pages. As you read
them, you may find yourself thinking, *I wish I could have met
him.* The fact is, you can not only meet him, you can be
mentored by him. He can leave his mentoring fingerprints
on your life just as he has on so many others in the trenches
of the modern prayer movement.

Strong Hands

Armin was a man with unusually strong physical hands. In
his youth he played baseball and even considered playing in
the major leagues. He had an equally strong mind, which he
used to gain a major-league grip on vital biblical and theological issues. Most significantly, Armin used his hand strength
and mental strength to take hold of a bunch of "young bucks"
and shape their lives. He molded us, pounded us and left his
fingerprints all over our lifestyles and thought processes.

For this reason in the writing of his biography I have cho-
sen to let Armin speak in his own words as much as possible.
You will enjoy his winsome personality, his infectious sense
of humor, his perennial youthfulness, his hard-hitting,
in-your-face exhortations, his graciously kind manner and
his tenaciously tight theological thinking. In reading this
book, you may find far more than a story; you may find a
friend—and, more importantly, a rare mentor.

This book was born in the front row of Armin's memorial service. That day I discovered I was only one of many who were brought into his inner circle of friendship and whose lives have been permanently and profoundly impacted by this most remarkable man. There is room for you in this front row. "As iron sharpens iron, so one man sharpens another" (see Proverbs 27:17). As you read, you have the opportunity to hop up on the anvil next to us and have your thinking challenged, your convictions pounded and your faith strengthened.

A biography gives us a rare opportunity for life-on-life impact. This particular biography is arranged theologically rather than chronologically. We will have opportunity to think through valuable life-transforming issues which have shaped many of the outstanding Christian leaders of our day.

Maximum Impact

You are certainly free to continue reading this book alone. However, for maximum impact, you may want to consider forming a twelve-week study group with a handful of friends who share this common passion.

To read a book on the life of Armin Gesswein all alone would almost do injustice to everything for which he stood. He knew that the prayer movement, as well as our own spiritual growth, develops most effectively in community. For this reason, study guide questions are included at the end of each chapter, some for personal reflection and some for small-group discussion.

People are God's priority, and mentoring is God's method of shaping and developing people. Keith Anderson and Randy Reese describe it this way: "Spiritual mentoring is a triadic relationship between mentor, mentoree and the Holy Spirit, where the mentoree can discover, through the already present action of God, intimacy with God, ultimate identity as a child of God and a unique voice for kingdom responsibility."[2] This description of mentoring will ring true in the following pages as we get to know Armin Gesswein.

Tiger Woods has been ranked the number one golfer in the world. He has the unique ability to blow away the field. Yet despite his high standard of excellence, Tiger still spends hours with his personal coach, Butch Harmon, before every major tournament in order to refine his skills. Finding this pattern a little hard to understand, I asked my golf-pro friend, "Why does Tiger Woods need to take golf lessons? Isn't that overkill? He is already the best in the world." My friend's answer not only taught me about golf, but about life: "Only duffers don't need coaches."

When it comes to the inner spiritual disciplines, none of us want to be duffers.

This book is for you—

- If you want to move beyond a duffer's prayer life.

- If you want to learn from a master, a pioneer of the modern prayer movement.

- If you are tired of playing church, and want to see your local congregation regain vibrant spiritual health and power.

- If you want to be part of the new generation of intercessors and perhaps the final generation before the return of Christ.

- If you want to reach a lost world through a revived church.

Chances are you've never met anyone quite like Armin Gesswein. As much as possible, we will allow him to speak in his own words. Through the pages that follow, we will be quoting from personal letters, prayer letters, newsletters and excerpts from dozens of never-before-published manuscripts. We want to begin in Chapter One by introducing you to the vision that drove the man, that eclipsed the man and which certainly outlives him. Then in Chapter Two we will introduce you to the man himself.

Summary

- Prayer must be frontal, not peripheral.

- We will one day be surprised to learn the invisible interplay between the private little prayer meetings and the great big public results.

- If the Holy Spirit doesn't do it, there is nothing to it.

- Only duffers don't need coaches.

CHAPTER ONE

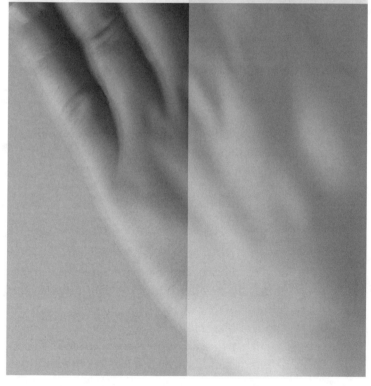

Prayer and the Upper Room

It was Jim Elliot who said, "I have determined for my life, wherever you are be all there; whatever you do, be *all in it*; and whatever you believe to be the will of God for your life, live it to the hilt." Armin Gesswein was the essence of that passion, to my view; compelled "to the hilt" to draw people to a life of commitment and devotion to Jesus—to service and to prayer. He achieved large influence because he was a large soul.

—Jack Hayford, Senior Pastor,
Church on the Way

Lord, send us revival without fanaticism—if you can. And if you can't, send us revival anyway.

—Charles Finney

When Christ ascended into heaven all He left behind was a prayer meeting. The early Church didn't have a prayer meeting; the early Church was the prayer meeting. In fact, in the early Church every Christian was a prayer-meeting Christian.

—Armin Gesswein

Many of us are familiar with an upper room. Normally it is an out-of-the-way place in our home where we store old golf bags, worn-out furniture or cardboard boxes full of stuff we don't use but don't want to toss. Or perhaps it is a rumpus room for kids to play in—a place where they can make a mess we don't have to look

at, or where they can practice on their drum set and we don't
have to listen. Sometimes it's a dark, cold and dreary room—
unused and unlived in.

Nothing could be further from the truth for Armin
Gesswein. For him the Upper Room was command central—
the busiest place in the universe, the most lived-in, exciting,
thriving place on either side of eternity. For Armin it was not
only a New Testament reality; it was a modern-day necessity.
Nothing more clearly illustrates Armin Gesswein's philosophy
of revival-prayer than the Upper Room. For this reason,
throughout the book we will spell it with a capital U and a capital R. And for the sake of brevity, we could refer to it as the
UR. Just as every local hospital has an ER, every local church
needs a UR.

Many theologians shy away from the book of Acts. Not
Armin. While he was always careful to differentiate between
the narrative and the instructive passages in the Bible, he
found a systematically logical basis for revival-prayer principles in Dr. Luke's second book.

> At Yankee Stadium I watched Babe Ruth
> hit a home run. Immediately I caught a
> vision. "You mean you can hit a ball like thaaaaat?"
> In the Gospels, I watched Jesus pray. Again I
> caught a vision. "You mean you can pray like
> thaaaaat?"
> —Armin Gesswein

His letter to me on February 16, 1989, cuts to the heart of
his Upper Room theology:

> The New Testament prayer meeting reveals the mas-
> ter plan of Jesus. The last thing Jesus did on earth was to

build that prayer meeting, and it is the only thing He left
behind on planet Earth when He ascended to heaven.
With this He unfolded His master plan for His Church,
for true Christian unity, for evangelism, for spiritual
awakening and revival, for dynamic church growth, for
birthing and battling, for the fulfillment of Acts 1:8.

We must never get away from the fact that when Jesus built His Church He built a prayer meeting. Everything He did led to it, and everything then came out of
it, much as a mighty oak tree comes out of a tiny acorn.
The prayer meeting embodies the embryonic secret of
the New Testament Church. Strangely, it is the best-
kept secret of the New Testament. Stranger still, it is the
most open secret. Jesus opens it up to our view more
fully than any other secret. The wonder is not that we
do not see it, but that we could fail to see it. So the problem is with our eyes. It is one of vision.

It is something which is so old that, when we discover it, it is new. This at once tells us that it is a secret
which has not changed. We must find our way back to
it. We must rediscover Christ's organic way of doing it.
And when we do, we will see wonderful awakening in
our churches.

Armin called the Upper Room "God's master plan for revival." He often reminded us that in the early Church every
Christian was a prayer-meeting Christian. Every pastor was a
praying pastor. Every leader was a praying leader. For Armin,
the book of Acts is the greatest book on revival which has ever
been written—greater than Jonathan Edwards or Charles
Finney or any of the others.

A casual acquaintance might mistakenly think Armin
Gesswein was driven by prayer. I don't think so. Rather he
was driven by a vision of what prayer accomplishes. More

specifically, he was driven by a vision of what prayer accomplishes out of the Upper Room.

"Make no mistake about it," Armin would often exhort, "the Upper Room was God's idea, not man's." He would then quote Acts 1:4 in his own words, "He commanded them not to depart from Jerusalem but to wait for the promise of the Father," pointing out that the word "command" or "charge" (Greek: *parangello*) was a military term that put them under orders. Jesus Christ literally commanded them to go to the Upper Room and establish a prayer meeting. Therefore, the Upper Room was instructive New Testament teaching, not narrative. While it may have been called an Upper Room because of its physical location on the roof of a private home, it was quite literally upper in importance, upper in priority, upper in value and significance. It was upper in the mind of Christ, who called for it initially in the first century, and it is to remain upper in the Church of the twenty-first century.

> The Upper Room is the masterpiece of history. He got it together and then He went to heaven.
> —Armin Gesswein

The Upper Room was not some afterthought. It was not a last-minute, last-ditch effort to salvage a weak, inept group of fledgling disciples. Jesus strategically trained His followers in prayer from the moment He called them, and in His final command He told them to go straight to the Upper Room as soon as He ascended into heaven. (We will see this concept unfold more clearly in Chapter Four, "The Prayer Life of Jesus," focusing on Jesus' strategic ministry plan in Luke's Gospel.)

Perhaps our trouble today is that we have not seen the Upper Room prayer meeting as a command of Jesus. Pastors seem to have little authority motivating their congregations into prayer meetings and showing them all that God wants to do there. Armin would often ask congregations, "If Jesus told you to go to prayer meeting, would you go?" He would always receive a roomful of affirmation. Then he would add, "Well, He did tell you to go! In fact He *commanded* you, right here in Acts 1:4." Using Acts 1:4 as his basis, Armin often called the central all-church prayer meeting "Christ's last command; our first responsibility."

Many evangelical Christians, particularly those with strong global missionary focus, mistakenly think Christ's last command was, "Go into all the world and make disciples of all nations," referring to Matthew 28:19. However, as imperative as Christ's command to go may be, His command to stay—stay and pray—was the final command, according to Dr. Luke.

Armin Gesswein saw that the Upper Room pattern holds the secret to all healthy church life. One little prayer meeting of about 120 in an Upper Room in the city of Jerusalem would launch the most revolutionary force ever to hit the world scene. Who would believe it? And there was no alternate plan.

> Pentecost didn't come through a
> preaching service; Pentecost came to a
> prayer service. From Pentecost to Patmos,
> God never departs from the pattern.
> —Armin Gesswein

At times Armin did sound like a one-string guitar. Without fear of exaggeration, I can say I have heard him teach from Acts 1 on the Upper Room prayer meeting at least 100 times. Like a good coach he did not mind taking us back to the basics over and over again. For Armin, the Upper Room was not an ancient relic from the annals of the early Church;

it was the driving force behind the Church through history and the only hope for the modern-day Church. Jesus put every other command and promise on hold for this last demanding commission. Armin succinctly summarized these thoughts in a personal letter to ministry friends. He comments on Acts 1:4, 14-15, "He [Jesus] commanded them not to depart from Jerusalem, but to wait for the Promise of the Father . . ." (NKJV). They obeyed, and "all continued with one accord in prayer and supplication . . . about a hundred and twenty. . . ." Sink your teeth into these juicy insights:

> God in His sovereign majesty has chosen to work by prayer. It is His eternal method. It is number one with Him. It was number one with Jesus when He was here on earth. He not only prayed about everything, He did everything by prayer. It is number one now with Jesus on the throne, where He "ever lives to make intercession for us" (see Hebrews 7:25). It is number one in His Church, for when He built His Church He built a praying congregation. When Christ built His Church He built a prayer meeting!
>
> It is impossible to improve on that pattern. It was not only made for the Jerusalem church, but for every church in the New Testament, from Pentecost to Patmos, and for every church since. The Lord gave His Church no other pattern. The early Church had glory and they had fire. When we depart from His template, we depart from His glory. We lose Holy Spirit fire and we begin to backfire and misfire.

The Upper Room was Jesus' master plan, which He masterminded to be the masterpiece and centerpiece of history. Moses commanded the tabernacle to be built "according to the pattern shown [to him] on the mountain" (Exodus 25:40). Jesus gave the blueprint for the construction of the Upper Room and we dare not devi-

ate from it: "Do not depart from Jerusalem, but wait for
the promise of the Father." Christ did not announce,
"I'm going to have a prayer meeting in Jerusalem and I
hope some of you will be able to attend it." No way. He
took upon Himself the role of the Commander-in-Chief
and used the strongest military term; He charged them
to go to the prayer meeting and that's all it took. They
all marched obediently right into the Upper Room. The
mandate from the Commander-in-Chief was all it took.

He worked so powerfully from that prayer meeting that the
Church exploded and the gates of hell could not prevail
against it. Christ demonstrated that He had "all authority in
heaven and earth" by building Himself an Upper Room prayer
meeting. The entire story of the book of Acts flows out of that
little prayer meeting.

Four Essential Upper Room Elements

It is possible that the Upper Room may sound more like an
abstract concept than a concrete reality. The word translated
"upper room" refers to a common and significant place in ancient Middle East residences. New Testament scholar R.C.H.
Lenski says, "Sometimes they were merely booths that were
erected on the porches of a stone building. . . . Sometimes they
were roomy and even ornate. . . . They were used as places for
retirement and quiet and for the company here described, as a
place that was free from interruption and disturbance."[1] To
help us get a better grip on it, it may be helpful to identify four
essential elements of the Upper Room. It should not surprise
us that each of these comes right from the book of Acts.

Essential Element #1: The Doorway of Obedience

As we have already identified, the Upper Room was not
only Christ's idea, it was His command (Acts 1:4). The only

thing Christ left behind when He ascended into heaven was a prayer meeting—an Upper Room prayer meeting—that took priority over every other church meeting. Just as an invitation by the President of the United States to attend an event at the White House takes priority over other social responsibilites, so an invitation from the King of kings and the Lord of lords to attend an Upper Room prayer service at your local church is to take priority over any other duty or obligation, whether personal, social or religious. It is not a matter of personal preference. It is very simply a matter of obedience.

To take the Upper Room beyond the individual and apply it to the corporate, each local church would do well to ask itself a few questions:

- Are we strategically giving Upper Room priority to training our people in corporate prayer?

- Are we obeying Christ's command to establish the corporate prayer meeting as the driving force behind our other local church ministries?

- Are we devoted to prayer the way first-century believers were?

The only doorway in the Upper Room is labeled "obedience." When asked, "Why are you coming?" we answer, "Because Christ commanded us to come."

Essential Element #2: The Atmosphere of Unity

Miracles did not begin happening after Pentecost; they began happening before Pentecost. One of the earliest miracles was the atmosphere of unity established among the 120 pre-Pentecost prayer meeting seekers gathered in the Upper Room. They not only gathered together, they gathered in one accord. Praying together like this brought the early believers into tight harmony. Like a great 120-piece symphonic orchestra, they were all working off the same score of music. God brought them into such tight unity that they became a living concert of prayer.

Prior to Pentecost it was said, "They all continued with one accord in prayer and supplication" (Acts 1:14, KJV). There was such intense unity among the 120 that when their numbers multiplied on the day of Pentecost and 3,000 were added, that same unity continued. The vision of the Upper Room prayer meeting was immediately caught by all 3,000. It says of them, "They devoted themselves . . . to prayer" (2:42).

Essential Element #3: The Ceiling of Spiritual Intimacy

As we cross the doorway of obedience into the Upper Room and discover the atmosphere of unity, we quickly realize the ceiling is actually wide open. Physically many Middle Eastern homes had open-air porches on the upper level. This paints a vivid picture of a spiritual principle illustrating for us that the Upper Room is a place of spiritual intimacy.

> "God never made anyone who
> couldn't pray . . . including you."
> —Armin Gesswein

The same Jesus who taught His disciples, "Do not . . . throw your pearls to pigs" (Matthew 7:6) was unwilling to pour out His precious Holy Spirit until He had a people prepared to receive Him. The true preparation of the disciples was obviously performed on the spiritual level. You can be sure Christ led these early Christians through deep repentance, brokenness and contrition in the days of pre-Pentecost Upper Room preparation.

The Upper Room provided such spiritual intimacy that the early church became *pregnant* in prayer. It can be said that the gestation period was ten days. Then the secret chambers of spiritual intimacy in the Upper Room became a birthing room on the day of Pentecost.

The old rabbis had a saying, "No birth without a pregnancy." They also said, "You can't be half pregnant!" The Upper Room in Jerusalem was perhaps the most prominent secret place in Scripture. Hidden away from the Jerusalem traffic the 120 early Christians continued in laboring prayer until the Holy Spirit was poured out on the day of Pentecost and the Church was birthed. Secret prayer is the secret of prayer. Jesus practiced and taught it: "Pray to your Father in secret . . . and He shall reward you openly" (see Matthew 6:6). All revivals are born this way—the Upper Room way. It remains the place of spiritual intimacy.

Essential Element #4: The Floorboards of Expectancy

The promises of Holy Spirit visitation became the spiritual expectation of the early believers. They rapidly moved from desperation to anticipation. It was in the Upper Room where the Spirit of God took the Word of God and used it to inseminate hope and faith into the people of God. The faith-building promises to which the local church clung certainly included the words which have been preserved for our faith-building benefit.

> But you will receive power when the Holy Spirit comes on you; and you will be my witnesses in Jerusalem, and in all Judea and Samaria, and to the ends of the earth. (Acts 1:8)

> If you then, though you are evil, know how to give good gifts to your children, how much more will your Father in heaven give the Holy Spirit to those who ask him! (Luke 11:13)

> And afterward,
> I will pour out my Spirit on all people.

Your sons and daughters will prophesy,
  your old men will dream dreams,
  your young men will see visions.
Even on my servants, both men and women,
  I will pour out my Spirit in those days. (Joel 2:28-29)

I am going to send you what my Father has promised; but stay in the city until you have been clothed with power from on high. (Luke 24:49)

But when he, the Spirit of truth, comes, he will guide you into all truth. He will not speak on his own; he will speak only what he hears, and he will tell you what is yet to come. (John 16:13)

As they knelt in prayer it was as if they were kneeling on a launching pad. Ten, nine, eight—we have ignition! "Suddenly a sound like the blowing of a violent wind came from heaven" (Acts 2:2). Seven, six, five—"They saw what seemed to be tongues of fire" (2:3). Four, three, two, one—"All of them were filled with the Holy Spirit" (2:4). We have liftoff! "Those who accepted his message were baptized, and about three thousand were added to their number that day" (2:41).

People think that revival is the last thing on God's big busy list—and therefore hard to get. It is not the last thing on His list—it is first. When He gives revival, He gives Himself.
—Armin Gesswein

Thus the mission of Christ was successfully initiated off the launching pad of prayer. The prayer place was called the Upper Room and it was characterized by the four elements of obedience, unity, spiritual intimacy and expectancy which brought them to the dynamic place of Holy Spirit visitation which God desires for every local church. This is what we commonly refer to as revival.

While we have more and more prayer for revival, how much revival are we actually experiencing? This was one of Armin Gesswein's chronic burdens. Just as an evangelist doesn't simply want to tell people about heaven, but wants to lead them to receive eternal life now, a revivalist does not simply want to pray about or talk about some distant revival; he wants revival now. In his booklet *Let's Have Revival Now: What Are We Waiting For?* Armin explained that the legitimate Upper Room is a birthing room where revival is born, not just talked about.

> Nothing, I suppose, is more prayed about or more needed than revival. And nothing is more promised in Scripture. Yet no praying seems to be so little answered. Most of the praying sounds as if revival is futuristic. We constantly hear the phrase, "when revival comes!" We futurize, generalize and depersonalize it. At times we are not even clear what we mean when we use the word "revival."

> The New Testament is never vague or general about it and it always begins with the local church. Pentecost was a church revival, then society felt the impact. Today too many of us are praying for society to be revived. We have it backwards. God cannot bring new life where there has never been life. On the contrary, it is the local church that is to wait on God's Spirit in order to be revived now. The kind of praying that brings revival is Upper Room praying. It was then and is now.

The level of expectation in the Upper Room gave them the faith to "pray through" until they received that for which they were praying. One day Armin explained to me that this was the difference between praying for revival and revival-prayer. "Praying for revival," Armin explained, "can push revival further and further off into the distance while revival-praying receives right now a portion of that towards which we are praying. It's just like when an individual receives by faith the infilling of the Holy Spirit. The only difference is that revival is a corporate infilling of the Holy Spirit."

Armin once asked me a very insightful personal question: "Fred, what good would it accomplish if you personally only prayed to be filled with the Holy Spirit, but never received? Wouldn't that be unfulfilling? Similarly, when we corporately pray for revival, it does little good if we never corporately receive." Praying through, then, is receiving while we are praying.

Upper in Priority

The Upper Room becomes the standard by which God holds every local church radically accountable. When God establishes the Upper Room, there is nothing He can't do through that local congregation. And until He establishes the Upper Room, there is nothing of greater priority. Establishing the Upper Room in every local church is number one on God's agenda.

Every local congregation has an Upper Room of one sort or another—a force that dominates. Unfortunately prayer is not necessarily that force.

Many issues jockey for the position of prominence in the local church. Churches are dominated by small groups, Sunday school, church planting, evangelism, counseling, benevolence or preaching. As important as each of these are, they do not merit dominance in the Upper Room. Jesus distinctly and emphatically said—with his white knuckles clenched around a whip, having just cleansed the Temple—"My house is to be a house of prayer." End of discussion.

The Brooklyn Gospel Tabernacle, under the pastoral leadership of Jim Cymbala, stands as a marvelous twenty-first-century example of a local church ministry driven by an Upper Room of prayer. In his book, *Fresh Wind, Fresh Fire*, he challenges individuals to "get uncomfortable" with an anemic prayer life. Citing Acts 2:42—"They devoted themselves to the apostles' teaching and to the fellowship, to the breaking of bread and to prayer"—Cymbala says we can't call ourselves New Testament Christians if we don't pray.[2] Armin Gesswein would completely agree.

> In the book of Acts they are praying in every chapter except two; and in those chapters they are in trouble.
>
> —Armin Gesswein

Twenty years prior to the birth of the modern prayer movement, Armin Gesswein wrote an article published by International Intercessors (1963) calling the church to reprioritize Upper Room prayer.

> We have forgotten that when Christ built His Church, He built a prayer meeting! We have forgotten that there was not a single member of that Jerusalem congregation who was not in the prayer meeting! We have forgotten that it advanced on its knees, all through the twenty-eight chapters of the book of Acts. We have forgotten that the place where they counted their numbers was in the prayer meeting. We have forgotten that united prayer was its supreme method for everything—that everything was done by prayer. We have forgotten that prayer was the very organizing principles of that Church: of its new oneness and unity of its officers, of its victory in battle against every form of persecution and opposition.

The book of Acts shows the intimate and unfailing connection between prayer and every work of God. "If God would do apart from prayer what He has promised to do in answer to prayer," Armin wrote, "then the very necessity of prayer would break down." But He does not. When God is about to do a work on the earth, He always starts by waking up His people and calling them back to Himself in prayer. When prayer is on the increase, all forms of prayer are reactivated and authentic revival is at hand.

In a handwritten note of exhortation, he offered the following challenge to me in 1996:

> Let's pursue until we get the Upper Room into every church, and until every church becomes the Upper Room. Our task is His task. It is time for some church to break into revival this year.
>
> In His love,
Armin Gesswein

The Mark of Authenticity

The Upper Room will never receive a *Good Housekeeping* Seal of Approval. It will not appear on the cover of *Better Homes and Gardens*. It may not be visited by kings, princes or heads of state. The Upper Room will, however, be visited by none other than Jesus Christ Himself in the person of the Holy Spirit, as promised in John 16:7-11:

> But I tell you the truth: It is for your good that I am going away. Unless I go away, the Counselor will not come to you; but if I go, I will send him to you. When he comes, he will convict the world of guilt in regard to sin and righteousness and judgment: in regard to sin, because men do not believe in me; in regard to righteousness, because I am going to the Father, where you can see me no longer; and in regard to judgment, because the prince of this world now stands condemned.

Most of us read past the little word "you." As Armin taught, however, that little word is the key word to God's law of revival. Let's paraphrase with appropriate emphasis. "When I send the Holy Spirit to you (first . . . to you my people . . . to you my Christians . . . to you my Church), then I will (through you) convict the world (the non-Christians around you) of sin, righteousness and judgment. . . ."

In revival, we are suddenly taken into the courtroom of heaven. The Holy Spirit is God's Advocate and summons our consciences to the bar of His judgment. At that point, the action of the Holy Spirit is twofold: The initial action in the Church and the subsequent action in society. This law of revival can be stated in a number of ways.

- The Holy Spirit brings conviction of sin to the non-Christian in the measure in which He first works in Christians in the Church.

- The unconverted feel their need of salvation when Christians first feel the need for them to be saved.

- When Christians feel their deeper need of the Holy Spirit, non-Christians will feel their need of Christ.

- The Church is first concerned for the world, and the world is concerned for Christ.

- Non-Christian seekers will deal with their sins according to the way Christians first deal with theirs.

- When Christians repent, sinners will repent.

- Sinners will pray and seek the Lord when Christians do so first.

- The unconverted will be "born again" of the Holy Spirit when Christians are burdened and birth them in prayer.

- When Christians are filled with the Holy Spirit, non-Christians will be convicted of sin and converted to Christ.

- When revival is strong in the Church, evangelism will be strong in the world.

- When Christians walk in the light they have, sinners will see the light in and through them.

- When God's people face the many plain Scriptures about holiness of life, cleansing from all sin, purity and victorious Christian living, sinners will face up to the plain Word of God regarding their salvation.

- When Christians wake up (revival), non-Christians will also wake up (evangelism).

This is what Armin Gesswein called "God's Law of Revival." It all flows from the Upper Room.

Prayer, as we have noted, is always primary with God. The first thing the Holy Spirit did on the day of Pentecost was to come to the Upper Room and fill the 120 believers. He formed the first New Testament church prayer meeting and answered their tremendous praying with an outpouring of Holy Spirit power. It is here where Jesus gives us the biblical basis for the local church prayer meeting. It was not optional; it was a command of Jesus. It set the pattern, the standard. The prayer meeting was the key to revival—and it still is. And it will be until Jesus comes again. It is important to see that the Holy Spirit did not fall on Jews all around Jerusalem in some kind of a general or generic outpouring. He came very intentionally and locally to that praying body in none other than the Upper Room.

> What we often called weakness,
> God calls wickedness.
> —Armin Gesswein

The Upper Room is central for the entire universe. It is man's open access to the throne room of God. It is the Holy of

Holies of the Christian experience. It is the most influential location a man is ever welcomed. It is the priority location where
Christ led His Church before He ascended into heaven. And it
is where Jesus lives today to make intercession.

The vision of the Upper Room is big. It's big enough for every
local church and every city church for all time. It's big enough to
transform your community and mine. It's as big as the throne
room of God and its influence is to the ends of the earth.

Summary

- The last thing Jesus did on earth was to build a prayer
  meeting.

- The Upper Room prayer meeting embodies the embryonic secret of the New Testament Church.

- In the early Church, every pastor was a praying pastor,
  and every Christian was a prayer-meeting Christian.

- The doorway that leads us into the Upper Room is
  the command of Christ (see Acts 1:4).

- The first miracle in the early Church was the unity of
  the 120 pre-Pentecost Christians.

- Just as many Middle-Eastern upper rooms (Greek
  hupperon) had no ceilings, the local church's Upper
  Rooms are wide open to the manifest presence of God.

- The mission of Christ was successfully launched from
  the launching pad of prayer.

- When God gives revival, He gives Himself.

- Revival always comes to the local church. God does
  not pour out His Holy Spirit in some generic way on
  unprepared people.

• God never does apart from prayer what He promises to do in answer to prayer.

• God's law of revival: Non-Christian seekers will deal with their sins according to the way Christians first deal with theirs.

Mentoring Group Discussion

1. What four or five qualities would you use to describe the Upper Room in the early Church?
2. How does the UR resemble an ER?
3. In what way is the Upper Room God's master plan for revival?
4. What specific promises were the early Church most likely praying for in the Upper Room?
5. What does it mean to "pray through"?
6. What revival principles are illustrated by the 1930 Oslo Revival?
7. Complete the following sentences:
    a. Revival is _____.
    b. A factor that is kindling revival in the Church today is _____.
    c. A factor that is hindering revival in me is _____.

CHAPTER TWO

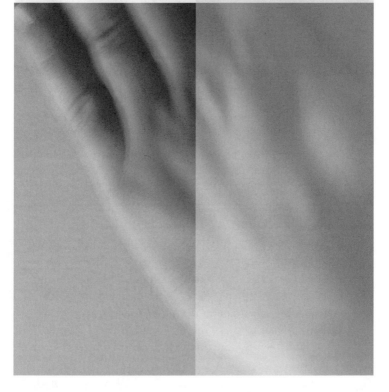

Prayer and the Man Himself

I thank God for Armin Gesswein. He was truly a man of God who listened to the voice of God, embraced the vision of God and responded to the call of God on his life. His vision for a revived Church has challenged me. His example, his writings and his prayers have touched me deeply. God be praised for such a life.

—Alvin J. VanderGriend,
Lighthouses of Prayer

Men are God's method. The Church is looking for better methods; God is looking for better men. . . . The Holy Ghost does not flow through methods, but through men. He does not come on machinery, but men. He does not anoint plans, but men—men of prayer.

—E.M. Bounds

Armin was unique. There are not many with the name, and even fewer with the winsome personality and infectious sense of humor. His monthly newsletter dated November 1996 is an engaging place to make his acquaintance.

I love Thanksgiving! Partly, I suppose, because I was born on Thanksgiving Day, November 28, 1907, in Corning, Missouri, not far from the Missouri River. This year it happens to come on my birthday again. And because I'll be eighty-nine this time around I'm even more thankful.

My father was a Lutheran minister in Bellingham, Washington, when my mother learned she was three months pregnant. Initially the doctor told mother she had a tumor. She was worried, and went to another doctor who smiled and said, "You better keep that tumor!" Mother went to Milwaukee where she had grown up, thinking she would have a good hospital for my birth.

It was Thanksgiving Day when someone told Mother, "There's a box social down the road a couple miles at one of our farmer's homes; would you like to go?" She went and toward evening she had labor pains. They quickly hitched up the horses and I had my first buggy ride. We rode not to the hospital, but back to the parsonage, next to the lovely brick church in the heart of the town.

And then guess what? My father had to deliver me! There was a doctor in the little town, but he was somewhere delivering a girl. My father was nervous. As a Lutheran minister he always prayed out of a book. But Mother said, "You should have heard him that day. He learned quickly how to pray without the book!" Soon the doctor came, and said to Dad, "You did all right!" And I guess it was a benign tumor. That was my first Thanksgiving Day!

I've thought two things about that day: (1) It was Thanksgiving Day, and I love thanks-giving. It's the one thing we can never overdo. I guess it is safe to say that I was born for thanks-giving. (2) Dad went into "free-praying" when he had to deliver me. So I think I was born for "free-praying." I also love praying with prayer books—especially the Bible, my *real* Prayer Book.

Mother's maiden name was Lydia Hilgendorf. While her sister Renata (Nettie) was there they asked her to suggest a name for me. She admired a young man in Milwaukee whose name was Armin. So I was named Armin. What a kind lady was our "Aunt Nettie." I was the second of six children, and we all grew up to hear from and admire and love our dear Aunt Nettie.

Virtually every piece of information Armin transmitted regarding his childhood is always sprinkled with joy and humor and the deep conviction that God was up to something in his own formation and development.

> There is not a Scripture that says,
> "Be sad." I looked for one but
> I couldn't find one.
> —Armin Gesswein

As a youth, he loved athletics, particularly baseball. He even tried out for the St. Louis Cardinals. Years later Armin declared, "God still talks to me in baseball language: 'Remember how you used to love baseball, and would rather play ball than eat? That's the way I want you to love and serve Me.' I understand that language." Eventually, he traded his baseball bat and gloves for a set of golf clubs, a game he enjoyed into his nineties. I watched him sink a thirty-foot putt for bogie in Norway at ninety-one years of age.

Although a Lutheran pastor, he came under conviction of sin and became convinced of his need for a Savior while listening to Paul Rader, a well-known Chicago radio preacher, declare, "What you need, poor troubled soul, is not some doctrine or creed or set of rites, you need to open your heart and receive the person of Christ into your heart."

That was the message that brought Armin to his knees. "Right there I said to myself, 'That's the way it is.' I received Christ as my Savior and Lord that day. I was born of the Spirit. Gone were my many doubts and my fears about sin. Like the pins going down when a bowler gets a strike, gone were my fears of death, hell, guilt. I walked around almost singing to myself, 'Now I'm born again.' "

Armin's ordination into Christian ministry was the next major event on record. His father recorded the event in his own handwriting.

> On August 2, 1931, I was privileged to assist in the unique and epoch-making event which consecrated my son and two other LaPorte County young men for pastoral office.
>
> We shall all talk about last Sunday's impressive evening service at St. John's many a time yet. And there is really much, so much to be said about it. Without fear of contradiction I can say, it was the happiest day and the most felicitous event that either St. John's or Trinity have had in all these six years, the first act of complete harmonious cooperation between the two churches. A new atmosphere is on tap, and the future augurs well. It is easy enough to see the guiding and directing hand of the "Shepherd and Bishop of our souls" in it all. To Him all praise and glory!

The Haystack Prayer Meeting

Several watershed events took place during Armin's first and only pastoral ministry in a Lutheran church on Long Island where he served as a young single pastor. The first event has been referred to as the "Haystack Prayer Meeting," perhaps Armin's first Upper Room experience:

> Early in the ministry I had an experience which completely changed my understanding of prayer. What a transformation! I was called to start churches and had just discovered "prayer-meeting truth" in the book of Acts. So I started a prayer meeting—the first one I ever attended.

In came an elder Methodist one night. When he prayed, I detected something new. "I have never heard praying like that," I said to myself. It was not only fervency—I had plenty of that. Heaven and earth got together at once when he prayed. There was a strange immediacy about it. The prayer and the answer were not far apart. He had it "in the bag!" being of optimistic faith. The Holy Spirit was right there, in action, giving him assurance of the answer even while he was praying. When I prayed, God was "way out there," somewhere in the distance, listening. The answer, too, usually seemed off in the distance.

Eager to learn his secret, I went to see him one day. His name was Ambrose Whaley, and everyone called him "Uncle Am." He was a retired blacksmith, a Methodist lay preacher. I soon came to the point: "Uncle Am, I would love to pray with you." At once he arose, led me outside across the driveway into a red barn, up a ladder, into a haystack! There, in some old hay, lay two big Bibles. I prayed first, as I recall it. Poured out my heart, needs, burdens, wishes, aspirations, ambitions to God. Then he prayed—and there was "that difference" again. There, in that hay, on our knees, at the eyeball level, I said: "Uncle Am, what is it? . . . You have some kind of secret in praying. Would you mind sharing it with me?"

I was twenty-four, he was seventy-three, and with an eagle-look in his eyes, he said, "Young man, learn to plead the promises of God!"

That did it! Those nine words have echoed in my soul a thousand times since: "Young man, learn to plead the promises of God!" My praying has never been the same since. That word completely changed my understanding of prayer. It really revolutionized it. Mentally I "saw it" as soon as he said it. Saw what? Well—when I prayed there was fervency, ambition, etc. And make no mistake about it, the Lord does not put a squelch on these either. But I lacked faith. Prayer is the key to heaven but faith unlocks the door. There must be faith. Where does that come from? From hearing the Word of God. Uncle Am would plead Scripture after Scripture, reminding Him of promise after promise, pleading these promises like a lawyer does his case, all along the Holy Spirit pouring in His assurance. This man knew the promises by the bushel. He did not seem to need those two Bibles in that hay. I soon learned that he was a mighty intercessor. He prayed clear through. He prayed through the Bible. He taught me the secret of intercessory praying. How can I ever thank God enough for leading me to such a prayer warrior?

What happened? With this discovery, God really gave me a new Bible! That day I learned how to make the Bible my prayer book. It gave me a new motivation for Bible study. I began to dig in. I would now search Scriptures . . . meditate . . . mark its many promises . . . memorize, memorize, memorize! There are thousands of promises for every need, burden, problem, situation.

"Young man, learn to plead the promises of God!" These words keep echoing in me.

The Prayer Meeting

The next significant, life-changing moment in the young pastor's ministry was the start of his corporate prayer meeting. Some of us have heard Armin tell this story dozens of times.

I saw the prayer meeting in the Bible. Jesus had them. The early Church had them. But we as good Lutherans didn't have them. Now I agreed with Luther: "Whatever is truly biblical is truly Lutheran." Since prayer meetings were in the Bible, I assumed they would be accepted. I arranged for a married couple in my congregation to host our first prayer meeting in their living room. I knew that

with them in attendance there would be at least three of
us present. I arrived five minutes before the prayer meeting was to begin. It was just the three of us. As I was about
to begin, another person arrived. I opened my Bible to
Acts chapter 1 and showed them the prayer meeting in
the Bible. I got on my knees, led in prayer, and to our
amazement it lasted all of five minutes. But it was a beginning. The next week there were eight and it continued to
grow. I had seen the prayer and healing services of Dr.
A.B. Simpson in New York City and I wanted that same
prayer power on our ministry. The more we prayed, the
more bold I became.

I went to a man in town who raised worms. He was
very poor and not very well educated. He smoked ciga-
rettes. I told him, "I have come to your house today so
you might receive Christ. I am going into the other room
and I will kneel down and pray for you. When you're
ready to receive Christ, let me know." It wasn't five minutes later that he came and stood at my side and said, "I
am ready." He knelt down with me and he received
Christ. He became one of the greatest prayer partners I
ever had. He couldn't speak well, so instead of asking God
to anoint the pastor, he would pray, "Lord, 'oint Pastor
Gesswein." I got more out of his "oint" than you would
ever imagine.

One day God said to me, "Armin, you
need to pray more." That shook me.
I prayed a lot about that. I realized
I had not lived up to the light
I had received.
—Armin Gesswein

The Communion Service

The third and undoubtedly most dramatic learning experience in the young pastor's life took place at a communion service. Around the Lord's Table Armin first tasted revival; it was that day God called him to a life of revival-prayer. Once he got his first taste, he never wanted to settle for anything less.

> Conviction of sin is the
> hallmark of true revival.
> —Armin Gesswein

We Lutherans always took communion seriously. But this one Sunday was categorically different. God convicted my heart over the sin within my congregation. People who came to church every Sunday had some of the worst reputations in town. They had been dishonest in their business dealings, prideful in their relationships and generally discrediting to the gospel of Christ.

On Sunday, the Lord's Supper had been prepared. It sat conspicuously on the communion table, front and center in the sanctuary. As I stood to preach I told the people with deep conviction and trembling in my voice, "Today I have a heavy heart. I am unable to serve us communion because of the obvious sin in our congregation. God would not be pleased with me or with you if we partook of the Lord's Supper in this condition. We are not ready to take the Lord's Supper. There is sin, even gross sin, in our church. God is a holy God and we must not come carelessly to His table. I call you to repent now from sin, to renounce it and to get right with God today. Then those who are ready will be allowed to receive from the Lord's Supper next Sunday."

You could have heard a pin drop. I knelt down in front of my chair. Others knelt in their pews. There was silence and there was weeping. People stayed there a long time. People openly prayed and confessed sin, made restitution, got right with people from whom they were alienated. God visited us that day in our church at the communion table.

As I stepped out the door that day, I heard the Holy Spirit say to me, "Armin, revival is your ministry." From that moment on I have not looked back. I never wanted to settle for anything less.

His Wife

Within a year Armin Gesswein was in the thick of Norway's revival. It was there he met the love of his life, Reidun Gabrielsen, who lived in a city named Tromso, 100 miles north of the Arctic Circle. On November 3, 1937, he wrote the following letter to his parents explaining his new relationship:

My dear Mother and Dad,

The time has come for me to let you in on a precious little love story. It is the thrilling romance of one who went all the way to the Land of the Midnight Sun and there found his bride waiting, prepared by Him who alone can make true love.

I felt I loved Reidun almost from the first look. It was different. She seemed to have the face and the whole personality and character I had looked for all over the world. It seemed to me to be the very God-given counterpart for me. Almost at once others noticed that we fit together long before we went out of our way toward each other or even spoke to each other more than to any others. So rare is our relationship that even imagination fails at this point to say nothing of poor reason with its slow heavy processes. But now I must watch myself and use language chaste and choice, for the paragraphs can easily become longer.

I am staying with Reidun's family. Their home is on the second and third floors over the store. We are announcing our engagement this week. That's why I am writing you this letter.

The Norwegian custom is to give the rings at the time of public announcement of the engagement. They are the wedding rings so no special engagement ring is necessary. We like that because we love simplicity. It is to the public announcement of engagement that family and friends are invited for the evening. This will be done this coming Saturday night at their home.

Her father is not living, sorry to say. Died suddenly a few years ago. He was only a couple of years younger than you. What a marvelous man he was. I have heard him spoken well of all over Norway. A keen man. Immensely practical. A rare business person and remarkable Christian. It was a tremendous blow when the Lord took him so suddenly. The mother is living. She is so sweet. And there are seven children, four girls and three boys. Two of the girls are already married, one to a Lutheran preacher and the other to the Bishop's son in Oslo. Reidun is the third child of the family. She is now twenty-four years of age. Her birthday is August 18. She's a precious girl, rare indeed. An outstanding Christian with unusual insight into the Word and the things of God. And so practical. Since her father's death she has been head of the business. And of course, as you may guess, she is also a pretty girl.

I shall try not to describe it all here. Hope to send you a picture soon. I don't know just when the Lord will have us get married, perhaps not for many months yet. I have places to visit and I am busy in the Lord's work. The Lord will yet use her here in her family business. Her brother, Leiv, will be twenty-one and soon take charge of the business. She has another older brother

who is not a Christian, or shall I say not yet. A wonderful family. It is happy again to be in such a warm family
circle pulsating with life. Perhaps next year the Lord
will let us marry and then come to America together.
Reidun is writing a little letter in English for you. So
you see, she knows a little English. She studied it two
years in high school. You will love her, I know. Of
course, you know she can't express her real thoughts in
any full manner in our language. Not yet. But we
thought it would be nice for her to write a line, however
simple.

Now I must close. So much to do these days. Write
me here. Having good meetings here. The Lord is blessing much.

Your loving son,
Armin

When Armin and his bride returned to the United States,
he took a professorship at Gordon Divinity School on the
East Coast and then at Fuller Theological Seminary on the
West Coast. It was there that his Orange County Pastors'
Prayer Fellowship in the greater Los Angeles area grew into
a force to be reckoned with. He attracted the regular partici-
pation of Richard Halverson (chaplain of the U.S. Senate),
Chuck Smith (pastor of Calvary Chapel), Harold Sala (president of the Guidelines ministry), Ted Engstrom (president
of World Vision) and others. He has crisscrossed our nation
for almost sixty years of itinerate ministry, consistently calling local churches to revival-prayer.

Ministry

Throughout his life Armin was himself mentored by select
men of great stature. "I spent a lot of time with A.W. Tozer," he
explained. "Whenever possible, we got together. I also drove

him around a lot. What times we had together—both in his south Chicago home and in prayer together under some tree at a C&MA camp meeting. As I recall, Tozer spent five hours in prayer entering into the Spirit's fullness and settled it all. . . . I believe it was his mother-in-law who sparked his inner plug on this."

A Gesswein favorite was George Mueller, who coincidentally also lived to be ninety-three years of age. Armin claimed to be mentored by Mueller's writings and by his lifestyle. In Mueller's own words,

> I would wait on God hours every day. I live in the spirit of prayer. I pray as I walk, when I lie down, and when I rise. And the answers are always coming. Tens of thousands of times have my prayers been answered. When once I am persuaded that a thing is right, I go to praying for it till the end comes. I never give up. Thousands of souls have been saved in answer to my prayers. I shall meet tens of thousands of them in heaven. The great point in prayer is never to give up until the answer comes. I have been praying every day for fifty-two years for two men, sons of a friend of my youth. They are not answered yet, but they will be. How can it be otherwise? There is the unchanging promise of Jehovah, and on that I rest. The great fault of the children of God is, they do not continue in prayer; they do not go on praying. They do not persevere. If they desire anything for God's glory, they should pray until they get it.[1]

Pastors' Prayer Fellowship

Armin loved his age. For him, being old was not a detriment in the slightest. Quite to the contrary, it gave him a platform of humor that endeared him to many an audience.

- "When I was younger they used to tell me, 'You're good looking'; now they say, 'You're looking gooooood.' "

- "People ask me, 'What's the secret of living long?' I tell them, 'Just don't die.' "

- "I hope to live to be 100 . . . because not many people die after turning 100."

Armin had a theory on retirement which he summarized in one word: "Heresy!" We affectionately referred to Armin as Caleb, quoting the verse, "As his days so shall his strength be." He wanted to finish the race well. And he did.

As you get older, you get younger on the inside.
—Armin Gesswein

In April 1956, *Christian Life* magazine carried a cover story on Armin Gesswein entitled "He Sparks Prayer for Revival." In Los Angeles, for instance, ministers gathered regularly to pray for revival. Prayer fellowship groups had been formed among pastors throughout the area. By 1949, Billy Graham's Los Angeles campaign was flooded with prayer. That campaign proved to be the first to capture general public attention. From this campaign Billy Graham's ministry has been catapulted into world prominence by the press, radio and TV.

The article stated,

> But citywide meetings aren't the goal of these pastors' revival fellowships. Rather, the purpose is revival at the level of the local churches, sparked by the pastors. Spurred by God's blessing in Los Angeles, Gesswein encouraged pastors in various parts of the country to meet regularly in prayer for revival. At first pastors were reluctant to expose themselves to the need for revival. To-

day, however, Gesswein feels the tide has definitely turned. Calls come to him from pastors of all denominations. "How can we start a revival prayer fellowship?" they query. "Do you definitely believe we shall see revival in our time?"

Gesswein responded, "Definitely. Ten years ago there was real question as to whether or not we would ever have revival again. Some said no. Others, 'We'd like to see it but it's impossible.' From some voices we heard, 'Prophecy is against it.' Meanwhile a few prayed. Today the possibilities of revival are generally accepted.

"The high rate of carnality and lukewarmness in our churches, if taken alone, argues that we are moving away from revival. But other factors show we are moving toward revival. Perhaps I should say it appears to be a movement of evangelism-toward-revival. To date, the movement of evangelism appears stronger in our country than that of revival. We need both. Scripture calls for both. I believe the second movement fulfills Scripture in the greatest possible manner. And I further believe that, before the Lord is finished, He will get us into the full movement of Scripture. Nothing less fulfills the Word, and nothing less has all the dimensions for all the need, in worldwide evangelization. In this view, all the movements of our day, including that of Billy Graham, are parts of a larger sovereign pattern to fulfill Scripture. 'God is using you,' people say. But my feeling is, 'God is working, and I'm just in on it.'

"The test of revival is, of course, the church. And the revival-barometer in the church is the prayer-life of the church. The Welsh revival, said G. Campbell Morgan, was a 'church revival.' The meetings were held in the church and chapel buildings all over Wales. Charles Finney always proceeded on the basis that a genuine revival begins in the church."

Armin's Humanity

Unlike many spiritual men, Armin never let you lose sight of his humanity. He was never caught up with himself. He was a man of genuine humility, a keen sense of humor and a passion for golf. Virtually everyone who spoke at his funeral had some warmhearted story to tell about Armin's golf game. Either the sinking of a long putt, an eagle or birdie or a come-from-behind back nine win. Armin was certainly a man of God, but he never forgot that he was just a man as well.

Summary

- I was born for thanks-giving.

- I was born for free-praying.

- God talks to me in baseball language.

- Young man, learn to plead the promises of God.

- I heard the Holy Spirit say to me, "Armin, revival is your ministry." From that day on, I've never wanted to settle for anything less.

- The revival barometer in the church is their prayer life.

- Every revival is a church revival.

Mentoring Group Discussion

1. Do I have an Uncle Am in my life?
2. What critical issue did Armin face with his denomination when he discovered the prayer meeting in the Bible?
3. What role did the communion service play in Armin's life? What role does the death, burial and resurrection of Christ play in maintaining the purity of revival?

4. What godly courtship principles do we learn from Armin and Reidun? How did he know she was a God-given counterpart?

CHAPTER THREE

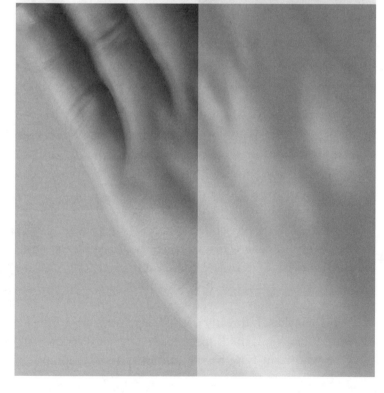

Prayer and Jesus' Teaching

Armin Gesswein was one of the greatest promoters of prayer and revival of the last fifty years or more. I have known him for almost that long, and have always been inspired and encouraged by his consistent focus on prayer.

—Bill Bright, Founder and Chairman,
Campus Crusade for Christ

When Christ built His church, He built a prayer meeting.

—Armin Gesswein

The boy's T-shirt reads, "Basketball is life." We can tell what is important to that junior high school student. The bumper sticker reads, "I golf for food." We know immediately the driver's priorities. If you were to reduce Armin's life philosophy to a bumper sticker or T-shirt it would probably read, "I live to pray."

Armin Gesswein was convinced that the greatest prayer we will ever pray is encapsulated in the disciples' straightforward request to Jesus, "Lord, teach us to pray" (Luke 11:1). Can you imagine? Five little words form the most profound, far-reaching prayer we will ever pray.

Lord. This takes us directly to the Master Pray-er. To the indwelling Intercessor, the King of kings and Lord of lords. To the One who right now has all authority in heaven and on earth under His dominion. If anyone can mentor us in prayer, it is He.

Teach. Instruct us. Give us both theology and methodology. Beyond that, inject Your prayer life under our skin and into our lifestyle.

Us. It's plural. It means corporate prayer: us, our children, our friends, our church family, the people we hang out with and with whom we share a common faith.

To pray. Don't just teach us about prayer; move us to pray—to the very act of it, to Your very throne. We won't settle for theory; we desperately want reality.

Just think: of all the activities Jesus engaged in—casting out demons, teaching, healing, walking on water, loving unlovely people—the only activity the disciples asked Jesus to teach them to do was to pray.

"Lord, teach us to pray." Yes, it's short and simple. It is one of the few bull's-eyes of life. Regarding this simple, five-word prayer Armin wrote,

> I'm 90 now. I have been involved in all kinds of churches and prayer movements for a long time. But a few years ago I began to pray this prayer and I'm amazed how much the Lord has opened up to me. Would you believe it? From this simple, plain Scripture which I had read many times yet missed, God is now taking me to school. That is very humbling. Yet I have now experienced wonderful new answers I don't have space here to tell. The Lord will do no less for you. Try it—you'll like it!
>
> I often say: Prayer is not everything, but everything is by prayer. If God wants us to pray about everything, He wants to answer prayer in everything. This He will teach us in His unique school of prayer.
>
> If someone offered me a million dollars, I would be very interested—and quickly! (Does anyone reading this

want to try me out?) But, realistically, what is a million dollars compared to what Jesus offers to give and do in answer to believing prayer? Promises like: "Whatever you ask for in prayer, believe that you have received it and it will be yours" (Mark 11:24, NEB).

When it comes to prayer, Scripture reveals how far we can go with God and also how far He will go with us. The prayer-promises are the plainest and most powerful promises in all the Bible.

Americans are supposed to be smart people. I mean, they usually recognize a good deal when they see one. If we are smart, we'll want to learn to pray. Nowhere does God promise more.

> Thou art coming to a King,
>   Large petitions with thee bring;
> For His promises are such
>   None can ever ask too much.[1]

In response to the disciples' simple five-word prayer, Luke 11 records that Jesus gave three helpful gifts in response: (1) a prayer pattern (11:2-4); (2) a prayer picture (11:5-8); and (3) a prayer principle (11:9-13). He intended them to put these gifts to good use.

> Prayer is so major we dare not
> minor on it any longer.
> —Armin Gesswein

The Gift of a Prayer Pattern

The Lord's prayer pattern recorded in Matthew's Gospel contains only fifty-two words. It can be said in a matter of seconds. It is the only pattern given to us by our Lord to use as a template when we pray. Yet, for the most part, neither Protestants nor Catholics understand how to put it to good use. Nevertheless it contains all the essence of spiritual intimacy. All the DNA necessary to spawn authentic spiritual life is found in these verses.

Track #1: Relationship—"Our Father in heaven . . ."

Christ makes it clear that we are not praying *for* a relationship, but *from* a relationship. We don't pray so that God will love us more; He already loves us as much as He ever will. He wants us to begin each day and each prayer with a conscious awareness of His love and blessing toward us. If we get no further than to allow our souls to marinate in His love, it will be a profitable prayer time. For this reason, the pattern begins, "Our Father."

Track #2: Worship—"Hallowed be Your name. . . ."

We quickly move from relationship to worship. The key to worship is a proper understanding of the name and character of God. Focusing on, praying, even declaring the names of God is the essence of worship. It is essential as we continue in prayer, flowing out of our love-relationship with the Father, to move into worship that is Christ-centered and Christ-exalting. We want to learn the names of God—to appreciate them, to pray and declare them, to value and cherish them.

Track #3: Lordship—"Your kingdom come, Your will be done on earth as it is in heaven. . . ."

Lordship completes the three "Your" statements—"Your name, Your kingdom, Your will." Henry Blackaby's *Experiencing God* course defines one of the spiritual realities as "God speaks by the Holy Spirit through the Bible, prayer, circumstances and the church to reveal Himself, His purposes and His plans."[2] "To reveal Himself" is to pray, "Your name be hallowed." To reveal "His purposes" is to pray, "Your kingdom come." To reveal "His plan" is to pray, "Your will be done." This moves from the higher part of the prayer, "Your name," to the principles, "Your kingdom," to the specific plans, "Your will."

Too many of us begin our prayer time praying for plans instead of God's purposes, let alone the higher plane of His Person. When we pray according to God's prayer template, He has us beginning where we should, firmly rooted in His Person. He then moves us to consider His principles, so that finally we can better pray His plans. Praying the three "Your" statements— "Your name, Your kingdom, Your will"—firmly places us subordinate to the will of God, inviting the reign of Christ.

Track #4: Sonship—"Give us today our daily bread. Forgive us our debts. . . ."

Two things a child asks his daddy for are food and forgiveness. For this reason we call this the "sonship" part of the Lord's prayer pattern. God loves us to look to Him as our Provider and our Forgiver. "And forgive us our debts" is the "speed bump" of the Lord's Prayer. We can be cruising along in prayer through other elements, but when we come to confession of sin it causes us to pause and take deeper inventory. The exhaling of sin and the inhaling of God's forgiveness makes for healthy spiritual respiration.

Track #5: Fellowship—"As we also have forgiven our debtors. . . ."

Certainly sonship and fellowship, even as receiving forgiveness for our sins and extending it to others, go hand in hand. Guarding the soul against resentment and bitterness is critical to our own spiritual well-being. Having been forgiven much, we are able to forgive others as well.

Track #6: Leadership—"And lead us not into temptation, but deliver us from the evil one."

In some ways, the whole prayer builds up to this point. How can we properly ask God to deliver us from the evil one if we have not confessed our sins, or if we hold unforgiveness in our hearts against others? Bitterness is one of the primary strongholds the enemy uses to gain ground and influence in our lives. It is healthy for us to daily put on the whole armor of God, submit to God and resist the evil one. For this reason the Lord Jesus included this portion of His prayer pattern.

The Gift of a Prayer Picture

After giving this prayer pattern, Jesus told the story of the friend who came at midnight who was hungry and homeless (Luke 11:5-8), illustrating the three levels of prayer: asking, seeking and knocking. The man who came at midnight did all three. Had he quit at level one or two, he would never have gotten the bread. But he demonstrated persistence, insistence—even obstinance. As Armin often said, tongue in cheek, "The man didn't have bread but he sure had crust!"

Though he began by asking for just three loaves of bread, by the end his friend was willing to get up "and give him as much as he needs"—far more than three loaves! This is the way it is with the deeper answers to prayer. God gives us even more than we ask for.

"True prayer doesn't start with us; it starts with God. The only prayer that reaches the throne, started there."
—Armin Gesswein

The Gift of a Prayer Principle

Whenever Jesus, the Master Teacher, told a parable, He painted a word-picture for a specific purpose. In this case, it was to highlight the three major words of summary: ask, seek and knock. These are three ever-increasing levels of prayer.

Level One: Ask-Praying

Armin taught that this is entry-level praying, where answers come quickly and easily. It is here where God encourages us to pursue Him in greater intimacy by giving us initial answers to prayer. Like a parent with small children, He looks out for every need we have and supplies us freely.

Level Two: Seek-Praying

This is deeper. Answers are slower and harder to come by. As we endure through trials, testing and discipline, our faith muscle grows strong. We wonder, *What is happening? Why is it taking so long? The Lord doesn't seem to be listening. I thought He loved to answer prayer.* Armin would answer,

> The problem is not with the Lord—it's with me. He has to work me over for the great things: getting me ready, bringing my faith to a higher level. Great things must be preceded by a greater desire. He doesn't want us running off like spoiled children; we would not be ready for them. God wants to humble us so that when the greater answers come, He receives greater glory.

Level Three: Knock-Praying

This is the deepest level; it goes to the very depths of our being. We are pleading—not prevailing against God's reluctance, but importuning His willingness. We can all naturally ask, "If God wills something so strongly and promises it so plainly, why do I need to plead so desperately?" Armin explained it this way:

> Again the problem is with me. God knows me better than I know myself. Do I really have the faith? Am I ready for this to happen? Have I really narrowed my sights? Do I really want the answer or not? This praying brings me into the Holy of holies. This is the bull's-eye. This is where answers are slowest in coming, where we are tested to the limit, but where the answers are the greatest. They may be few and far between, but well worth the wait.
>
> The Bible is full of this kind of praying. Abraham prayed for years, receiving many lesser answers to prayer until he received the big answer of his life: Isaac. Why did he have to wait so long? Why was he so tried and tested, disciplined and developed? Hebrews 11:12 says Abraham was as good as dead. That's right—dead to Abraham! He was dead to self: to self-reliance, self-effort, self-advancement, self-sufficiency. He was definitely as good as dead. This is a perfect description of knockers.
>
> Jacob also wrestled all night with God until God changed his name to Israel. This level of knock-praying is where God hammers His character deep into our lives to prepare us for the greatest answers to prayer. It so changed Jacob that he needed a new name.
>
> Then of course we remember the 120 in the early Church who learned this third level of knock-praying. God prepared them for a mighty visitation.
>
> Bottom line: Jesus shows here that the major answer to prayer which He desires to give to His Church is the Holy Spirit. "If you then, though you are evil, know how to give good gifts to your children, how much more will your Father in heaven give the Holy Spirit to

those who ask him?" (Luke 11:13). Jesus spoke this
word as the bottom-line answer to the five-word prayer,
"Lord, teach us to pray." The only way to learn to pray
is to be taught by the Holy Spirit. This was true in the
first century and in the twenty-first century.

What this means is that Pentecost-like revival was never intended to be a singular event in church history. Rather, it was
intended to be a continual event. It was intended to take the
Church into ever-expanding concentric circles of influence, to
span the globe as well as the centuries. To put it more simply,
Holy Spirit revival is the norm for the local church.

Plain Scripture and plenty of it.
—Armin Gesswein

Many who teach prayer principles shy away from the
plainest prayer promises because they seem so explo-
sive—almost embarrassingly so. Not Armin. He loved them;
in fact he scolded us for hardly ever taking a good look at
them. When it comes to these seven, he seems to call our
bluff. He said that the following seven prayer promises
"form a whole constellation in the kingdom of heaven."

"Whatever you ask in My name, that I will do, that the
Father may be glorified in the Son" (John 14:13, NKJV).

"If you ask anything in My name, I will do it" (14:14,
NKJV).

"If you abide in Me, and My words abide in you, you
will ask what you desire, and it shall be done for you"
(15:7, NKJV).

"You did not choose Me, but I chose you and appointed
you that you should go and bear fruit, and that your fruit
should remain, that whatever you ask the Father in My
name He may give you" (15:16, NKJV).

"Most assuredly, I say to you, whatever you ask the Father in My name He will give you" (16:23, NKJV).

"Until now you have asked nothing in My name. Ask, and you will receive, that your joy may be full" (16:24, NKJV).

"In that day you will ask in My name" (16:26, NKJV).

These promises are very powerful. Why do we quit on them? Are they too good to be true? Let's ask a deeper question: Does the Lord Jesus Himself seem to quit on them? Does He appear in any way to be reluctant to fulfill them? "Not at all!" Armin answers.

On the contrary, God longs to do just what He says. In fact, these great and precious promises are the ones He puts first, and the ones He wants to fulfill most of all. He gives them priority.

What do we do? Just when we face these golden prayer promises we quit. It's hard to believe, but just when we are in sight of the gold we have always wanted, we quit. It would be like having the gold-fever and going all the way west in the gold-rush days, when suddenly we see some big nuggets on the face of the ground right in front of our eyes. We wouldn't even have to dig or gold-pan a stream for them. There they are. More than we ever dreamed of on the long westward journey. And then we quit. Can you believe it? Instead of quickly laying hold of them, we don't even bother with them.

That's what we do with these exceeding great and precious promises. There they are, and we just let them lie there! The answer to everything we need or desire or are made for. They are given to make us rich in Christ: rich in good works—the wonderful works of the Holy Spirit—rich in every kind of answer to prayer. But we hardly pay any attention to them. This is so hard to believe.

We could become very strong in prayer; instead we quit and remain weak. We could experience great answers—life-changing answers—but we quit. We could have great prayer meetings in our churches, but we quit going, or don't even have prayer meetings. Our assemblies could be full of people, full of power from on high, but we have forsaken the assembling of ourselves together (Hebrews 10:25). We could be victorious Christians—overcomers against sin and Satan, but instead we quit, become undercomers and live defeated lives. Let's repent of our quitting prayer—quitting on the plain Word of God, quitting on the Lord Himself!

The effectiveness of our prayer life is measured by the size of our answers.
—Armin Gesswein

Armin loved to return to Luke 11:1. Like a salmon to its spawning grounds, he would frequently swim back upstream to the headwaters of the gospel narrative and read, "Now it came to pass, as He [Jesus] was praying in a certain place, when He ceased, that one of His disciples said to him, 'Lord, teach us to pray, as John also taught his disciples' " (NKJV). Armin commented on this passage as follows:

> This raises some great questions: Who? When? Why?
> *Who* asked this of Jesus? They were not backsliders, nor were they kindergarten believers. They were Jesus' disciples—some of the strongest praying people on earth. They had paid the full price, given their all to follow Jesus. We should not feel childish praying this prayer.
> *When* did they pray this prayer? Not at the beginning, but late in their life with the Lord, after about three years of being with Him. In fact, there were only about four months left of Jesus' earthly life and ministry. Finally, His

great prayer-life caught up with them. Their eyes and ears were fully open to the enormous things that happened when Jesus prayed.

Why did they now pray this? This is the big question, and it raises more questions. Why would some of the strongest-praying people in the world ask this of Jesus at this late date, after three years with Him to teach them to pray?

Let's consider how strong they were in prayer already. We would think they had arrived. They had already learned prayer through John the Baptist, the greatest praying man of his time. And now they had been with the Master Himself, learning for three years and getting some mighty answers. They had been on all kinds of evangelistic tours with Him and on their own. They had seen all kinds of healings, and had power and authority to cast out demons. They had prayed the Lord of the harvest to thrust forth laborers into His harvest (see Luke 8, 9, 10).

This was powerful praying. They were in the thick of miracles every day; their prayers were being answered. Even so, compared with the glorious things which happened when Jesus prayed, they realized they had only begun. They wanted to pray like He prayed and get answers like He got.

If you only pray on the run, you run out.
—Armin Gesswein

If you and I want to see the full potential and power of prayer, we must see into the prayer-life of Jesus. It was the golden secret for everything He said and did. He did indeed teach them to pray like He prayed. By the time He died for their sins, rose again from the dead and ascended to heaven, they really did know how to pray. He made sure of it. The book of Acts reveals it fully. His greatest secret—how to pray—now became their greatest achievement. The prayer life Jesus instilled in His disciples became the launching pad of the most far-reaching mission in world history. And it was launched from the Upper Room.

What a lesson for us! The "praying-est" people on the face of the earth—the disciples, who really knew something about prayer and answered prayer—were the ones who really wanted to learn to pray. They knew it was the golden secret and they went after it like gold in the gold rush. Make no mistake about it: Jesus' prayer promises are loaded!

The prayer teaching of Luke 11 began with the simple yet all-inclusive request, "Lord, teach us to pray" (11:1) and ended with Jesus teaching them to receive the Holy Spirit as they pray (11:13). In other words, He taught them revival-prayer. He taught them that the essence of prayer was to receive the promise of God, the Holy Spirit, and that everything else would flow from there. To learn to pray is to learn to revival-pray. What a lesson!

Do you know what the greatest prayer is?
"Lord, teach us to pray." Because when
we learn to pray we can receive
anything from God He wants us to have.
—Armin Gesswein

Summary

- "Lord, teach us to pray" is the most important prayer we will ever pray.

- When we learn to pray, there is nothing we can't receive that God wants us to have.

- When the disciples asked to learn to pray, they were taught to revival-pray.

- If God wants us to pray about everything, He wants to answer about everything.

- God doesn't want to raise spoiled children.

- Pleading prayer is not prevailing against God's reluctance, but learning to importune His willingness.

- God knows me better than I know myself.

- It is at the level of knock-praying where God hammers His character deep into our lives.

- Pentecost-like revival was never intended to be a singular event in church history.

- The disciples, the "praying-est" people on earth, were the ones who came and asked Jesus to teach them to do it better.

Mentoring Group Discussion

1. Why is it said that the most important prayer is, "Lord, teach us to pray"?
2. What did that five-word request reveal to us about Jesus? About His disciples?
3. How did Jesus respond to their request?
4. Why do we often shy away from the plainest prayer promises?
5. Can you identify with the term "quitter pray-er"?
6. As a group, take thirty minutes and use the Lord's prayer pattern. Have one person in the group announce the beginning of each of the six tracks; allow approximately five minutes of group prayer for each track.

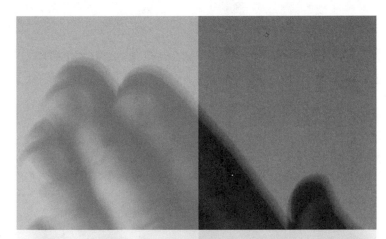

CHAPTER FOUR

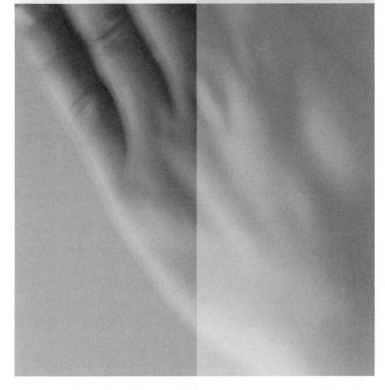

Prayer and Jesus' Example

Armin didn't only live a long time, he lived well—very well. For many decades he was one of the key prayer leaders of the world. In a group he was the first on his knees and the last to get up. Time after time I had breakfast with Armin just to soak up his heart for revival. Whenever we met I always took with me a pad of paper to take notes. As we chatted, he never put people down. He was positive and loving of all the body of Christ. Anne and I, too, are burdened for revival. Armin and Reidun were our mentors who inspired us to go after the revivial of God's people—with prayer, and as he put it, "lots of it!"

—Raymond Ortlund
Renewal Ministries

Just watch: Jesus will change the world with that little prayer meeting. Revival in the church is as near as our prayer meetings.

—Armin Gesswein

God can refuse nothing to a praying congregation.

—John of Chrysostom

I was spellbound—riveted on every word. Sitting in the front row, listening to Armin teach on Jesus' prayer life from the Gospel of Luke, I was "in the zone." Or, should I say, he was "in the zone." I had read through Luke a

dozen times, but somehow I had missed it. Oh, I had read
the verses, but I missed the point. I had missed the strategic
method Jesus effectively employed to build prayer into His
followers and prepare them for the Upper Room.

Behind me were seated over a hundred members of my
church who came to our "School of Prayer" on a Monday night
to listen to Armin Gesswein lecture for an hour. I was so absorbed in the content of his teaching and the fresh accuracy
with which he taught that I became oblivious to anyone else. I
was catching a vision that would change my life. For the first
time I understood that the concept and blueprint for the Upper
Room was in Jesus' mind from the moment He said to His first
disciple, "Come, follow Me." The result would be to become
fishers of men. The path would take them to the ends of the
earth, but it was all via the Upper Room.

Let's allow Armin to give us a no-frills, bird's-eye view of
Jesus' strategic prayer training which led His followers to the
Upper Room. Feel free to open your Bible and come along.

I had previously done Bible studies in the Gospels on Jesus' prayer life. I had noticed passages such as:

> Very early in the morning, while it was still dark, Je-
> sus got up, left the house and went off to a solitary
> place, where he prayed. (Mark 1:35)

> One of those days Jesus went out to a mountainside to
> pray, and spent the night praying to God. (Luke 6:12)

> But Jesus often withdrew to lonely places and prayed.
> (Luke 5:16)

The role model Jesus gave us as a man of prayer is a powerful and life-giving example. However, what Armin shared
with us this Monday night took Jesus' model to a higher
level. It was not simply Jesus the Pray-er, but Jesus the

Prayer Meeting Builder, who only ever builds one kind of church—a praying church.

Resist the temptation to speed-read this material, or worse yet to skip to the next chapter. In fact, I invite you to open your Bible and take some notes.

Luke 1:8-10—Zechariah, John the Baptist's father, was a man of prayer. He was a priest, a prayer leader in his own right who displayed considerable influence in mobilizing prayer. "All the assembled worshipers were praying outside" (1:10).

Luke 1:13—John the Baptist was born in answer to his parents' prayer. What a tangible, graphic, down-home example of birthing-prayer. John the Baptizer would have been told through his childhood and adolescent years, "You are an answer to prayer. Your daddy and I were unable to conceive but God heard our heart cry."

Remarkably, Zechariah not only recognizes the angel of the Lord, but he listens to him, talks to him, questions him and humbly obeys him. (While Zechariah at first questions the validity of the angel's report, and is rebuked and disciplined, his later actions show true repentance for his initial unbelief.)

Luke 1:26ff—Mary sees and recognizes the angel Gabriel. She too listens, questions and obeys the voice of God through His angelic messenger. While an angelic visitation is certainly not an everyday occurrence, even for a devout praying person, her response to the angel demonstrates a well-developed spiritual inclination.

Luke 1:46-55—Mary shows herself to be a mighty woman of prayer. Her song demonstrates a deep, mature, well-developed prayer fellowship with God.

Luke 1:67ff—When John was born and his name announced, his dad spoke an extended prophetic prayer. This too reveals a mature, well-developed prayer life.

Luke 2:26—Simeon, who recognized Jesus, had such a well-developed prayer life that he was able to accurately recognize the voice of God. Additionally, he was spiritually sensitive and responsive; he was "moved by the Spirit" at the precise moment that baby Jesus was brought into the temple for circumcision. The public prayer he spoke represents not only a profound theology, but an authentic and passionate spirituality. Simeon was obviously a man of prayer.

Luke 2:37—Anna, who recognized Jesus, was a woman of prayer. She lived to pray. Day and night she prayed. In a sense, she never came up for air—prayer was her air. Is it any wonder that God not only gave her the joy of seeing Christ face-to-face, but also the profound revelation of whom she was seeing?

Luke 3:21—The Holy Spirit descended on Jesus at His baptism "as he was praying." Luke is the only Gospel writer who shows this connection between praying and heaven being opened. This moment was a foreshadowing of the Upper Room of Pentecost when heaven was opened and the Spirit descended on Christ's body, the Church, "as they were praying."

Luke 4:1-2—Jesus began His ministry with forty days of fasting and prayer. It is easy to superficially dismiss the fact that Jesus' first act, at the start of His public ministry, was prayer. He prioritized prayer as His first work; His entire life ministry flowed out of His prayer life. This is the same pattern He would later set for His Church.

Luke 5:16—"But Jesus often withdrew to lonely places and prayed." For Jesus, prayer was not merely some-

thing He did; it was a lifestyle. He too lived to pray.
Talking with the Father, listening to the Father, taking
His lead from the Father, was His *modus operandi*.

Luke 6:28—Jesus told His followers to pray even for
their enemies. Prayer puts everything in proper perspective and taps us into His sovereign plan not only for
us, but for the world around us.

Luke 9:29—The Holy Spirit covered Christ with a
cloud of glory on the Mount of Transfiguration "as he
was praying." Again the Gospel of Luke uniquely contains this detail. Once again we see the connection between the glory of God being manifest and the activity
of prayer.

Luke 10:2—As Christ sent out the seventy disciples as
short-term missionaries, He exhorted them, "Ask the
Lord of the harvest . . . to send out workers." Christ is
drawing a line in the sand and saying unequivocally
that the fulfillment of our mission on earth is directly
proportionate to our prayer life (i.e., the work of God is
done by prayer).

Luke 11:1—"One day Jesus was praying in a certain
place. When he finished, one of his disciples said to
him, 'Lord, teach us to pray, just as John taught his disciples.' " Here Jesus' mentoring moves to a categorically
higher level. He now has them eating out of His hand.
They are coming with a longing inside their bellies to
learn to pray.

   In addition we learn some further valuable information about John the Baptist. Having seen the major role
prayer played in his birth (Luke 1:13) and in his home
life (Luke 1:8, 67ff), we now learn that he too carried on
such a relevant prayer life of his own that he intentionally and systematically taught his own disciples to pray.
In fact, we have no record of John ever teaching his fol-

lowers to baptize or preach, but we know he taught them to pray.

Luke 11:2-4—Jesus gives them a prayer pattern, a prayer template.

Luke 11:5-13—Jesus gives many powerful prayer promises.

Luke 18:1-8—"Then Jesus told his disciples a parable to show them that they should always pray and not give up." This verse contains two absolutes: "always" and "never." Jesus said His followers should *always* pray, and *never* stop praying.

Luke 19:46—When Jesus boldly declared, "My house will be a house of prayer," He identified the single activity that was to be top priority when God's people gather. We can clearly see how passionate Christ was about the priority of prayer and corporate worship.

The point behind His reference to a "den of thieves" can easily be missed, however. Was Jesus accusing the vendors of price-gouging—robbing the worshipers at the temple? Not at all! Unethical sales practices may well have been going on, but Christ was not rebuking the vendors for selling, nor the worshipers for buying.

A den is not where thieves rob, but where they hide after robbing. Jesus was rebuking them all for hiding from God! They were going to the temple, the very place designed to meet with God, and were doing the exact opposite—they were hiding from God. With a bullwhip in hand, Jesus set straight the priority of His Church. As we gather, our primary corporate activity is to be prayer—prayer that brings us into an encounter with God. Church is to be a place to meet with God, not a place to hide from God.

Luke 22:32—Jesus tells Simon Peter, "Satan has asked to sift you as wheat. But I have prayed for you." Jesus' prayer life was always at least one step ahead of the enemy. Even when He had more than enough things on His mind, Jesus intentionally and strategically prayed for Peter—and He made sure Peter knew He had prayed. Do we pray for our disciples the way Christ prayed for His? How many have fallen away because we did not pray for them to persevere?

Luke 22:40-41—How did Jesus and His disciples spend their last night together? Sharing? Bible study? Eating? By now it should come as no surprise: Jesus exhorted His disciples to spend their final night with Him in prayer. The Mount of Olives became their open-air Upper Room.

Luke 23:34—Jesus prays from the cross, "Father, forgive them, for they do not know what they are doing."

Luke 23:46—Jesus again prays from the cross, "Father, into Your hands I commit my spirit."

Luke 24:49—The resurrected Jesus sternly exhorts His followers, "I am going to send you what my Father has promised; but stay in the city until you have been clothed with power from on high."

Luke 24:50-51—This is the final picture Dr. Luke shows us of Jesus: "He lifted up his hands and blessed them. While he was blessing them, he left them and was taken up into heaven." At this moment Jesus moved from one prayer meeting to another. He left the one He built into His disciples on earth and immediately stepped right into the one awaiting Him in heaven. Today, of course, He is still praying for us, since He lives to intercede for us (see Hebrews 7:25).

When I went home after our School of Prayer that night, I re-read Luke. As I marked a "P" in the margin of my Bible next to each verse which dealt with prayer, it became crystal clear that the Upper Room was no accident, no afterthought. The Upper Room was in Jesus' heart from the moment He first said, "Come and follow me."

The prayer life of the Lord Jesus Christ is the standard. His prayer life becomes the plumb line for all of us. He lived a life of prayer. More than that, He built His prayer pattern into His disciples, and, through the Holy Spirit, He reproduces His prayer life in us, His Church.

On the cross, He died praying.
He died as He lived.
—Armin Gesswein

When we returned on Tuesday night to the School of Prayer, Master-teacher Armin invited us to turn to Dr. Luke's second book—Acts. He noted that the first verse becomes a bridge between the two books: "In my former book, Theophilus, I wrote about all that Jesus began to do and to teach." By summarizing his Gospel as "all that Jesus *began* to do and to teach," Luke implies that the book of Acts contains what Jesus *continues* to do and teach.

Armin also showed us that the first chapter contains not one great prayer meeting, but two. Obviously the 120 believers were gathered in one prayer meeting on earth. What many of us miss is the second prayer meeting, conducted by Jesus Christ in heaven. Christ's Church was in the earthly Upper Room and Christ Himself was in the heavenly Upper Room. The first prayer meeting was full of believers, all in one accord; the second was full of angels, archangels and God Himself, all in one accord. As the true High Priest that He is, Christ took charge of both prayer meetings, the one in heaven and the other in Jerusalem.

It is not surprising to learn that Jesus so quickly answered not only the prayers of the 120, but His own prayers as well. As recorded in John 14:16-17, Jesus said, "I will pray the Father, and He will give you another Helper . . . the Spirit of truth" (NKJV).

Jesus had meticulously, scrupulously and effectively prepared His leaders, including Peter and the others, to lead this great new prayer meeting.

The "punch line" to this New Testament prayer principle is that Jesus is still occupying His Upper Room—and He expects us to occupy ours. Make no mistake about it: Jesus' entire discipleship ministry was to build an Upper Room prayer meeting into which He could pour out His Holy Spirit. Pentecost came to a prayer meeting—we seem to forget this! The 120 members were filled with the Holy Spirit only after waiting on God in a ten-day prayer meeting. The Holy Spirit did not fall on Jews all around Jerusalem in some kind of a general or promiscuous outpouring; He came exclusively to that praying body in the Upper Room.

John 16:7-8 is a frequently quoted and easily misunderstood prayer promise: "But I tell you the truth: It is for your good that I am going away. Unless I go away, the Counselor will not come to you; but if I go, I will send him to you. When he comes, he will convict the world of guilt in regard to sin and righteousness and judgment."

This passage is commonly used to generate prayer for God to pour out His Holy Spirit on the world to convict them of sin—but that is not what Jesus said. Armin pointed out two little words: "to you." They are the two words most frequently missed in this passage, but they are the hinge words of this prayer principle: "I will send him (the Holy Spirit) *to you.*" Jesus said, in effect, "I will not send the Holy Spirit to the world. That is impossible. They aren't prepared for the Holy Spirit. I have prepared you, My disciples, for the Holy Spirit. And when He comes with force on you, He will, through you, convict the world of sin and righteousness and judgment."[1]

After the Holy Spirit would come to the disciples, there would come a mighty explosion of Holy Spirit conviction on the surrounding culture. "When he comes to you, he will convict the world of guilt in regard to sin and righteousness and judgment" (John 16:8-9). The Holy Spirit does not leap-frog over the local church. He comes *to* the local church. He has no other venue from which to work. He came not just to any random local church; He comes to the *praying* local church.

When Peter preached at Pentecost to this mass of Jews, thousands were brought under conviction of sin, righteousness and judgment—to repentance, to conversion, to salvation, to immediate baptism. The Scripture says that these unconverted Jews were "pierced" in their hearts—the same Greek word used when the Roman soldiers punctured the chest cavity of Jesus on the cross. When the Holy Spirit came in fullness to the Church, conviction of sin hit those in society like a spear in the chest and they cried out in desperation, "What shall we do?" (Acts 2:37).

Peter preached a brand-new message: Christ the Messiah. He became the first revival preacher of the New Testament Church. The winning combination for revival in a church is strong praying and strong preaching—both are essential. Strong preaching will never pierce the hearts of people until there is also strong praying. "I have noticed through the years that strong preaching on repentance without strong praying backfires or misfires," Armin said. "Worse yet, there is *no* fire—only hardening of heart. There must be the right combination of both preaching and praying as shown by Peter at Pentecost."

The awakening was so powerful in Jerusalem that 3,000 Jews were converted to Christ and added to the 120-member congregation, all on the same day. That shows the enormous new power of the conviction of the Holy Spirit when He works in revival. The Pentecostal power of the Spirit displayed in the first New Testament congregation in Jerusalem was the greatest force on earth—even the gates of hell could not prevail against it.

The book of Acts—and the entire New Testament—makes it clear that we are to pray for and expect revival in the Church. Pentecost, after all, came to a local congregation. The Lord would never allow the Great Commission to be fulfilled apart from the praying, Spirit-filled congregation in the Upper Room. The same pattern Jesus used in Jerusalem in the beginning will be used to reach the final unreached person prior to His second coming. We will never finish the task any other way, because Jesus gave us no other plan.

Jesus said, "A man can receive nothing, except it be given him from heaven" (John 3:27, KJV). Armin offers up a powerful prayer principle from these words:

> It is very easy to miss the obvious. Man is the one being who is fully vertical. He is not an animal. He is the only being on earth created in the image of God, made for fellowship with Him. And he is the only being on earth who is made for prayer and answered prayer. And man is never taller than when he is on his knees before God. God's way up is down. A lady said, "God is not working in my life; nothing is coming down." Then she woke up to the fact that she was not sending anything up in prayer. Every drop of rain will tell you it somehow had to go up first before it came down. "You have not

because you ask not" (see James 4:2). The devil wins hands down if we do not lift our hands in prayer!

Christ alone is the completely vertical Person—the God-man. When He was on earth He did everything by prayer, and now He does the same thing from above on His throne in heaven. It has been said that Jesus was the most original Person Who ever lived. What a surprise in Scripture to find that He was not original at all! He never said anything more plainly: "I can of my own self do nothing"; "I do always those things which please the Father"; "I came not to do my own will, but the will of Him Who sent me" (see John 5:19-20; 8:29; 5:30). He did nothing on His own.

In one thing, however, He was original—most original! It was in His unique Sonship, in His complete obedience to His Father. He was original in that He did everything by prayer. All of His massive ministry—so full of mighty miracles and majestic words—was answer after answer to His great praying.

At the end—indeed, the night before He was crucified—He fully revealed His deep, lifelong secret. He said, "Do you not believe that I am in the Father, and the Father in Me? The words that I speak to you I do not speak on My own authority; but the Father who dwells in Me does the works" (14:10, NKJV). Here He also reveals that His words and works are one indivisible flame. Even His many disciples, He says, were all given to Him in answer to His praying: "I have manifested Your name to the men whom You have given Me out of the world. They were Yours, You gave them to Me" (17:6, NKJV). And finally, in this same prayer to His Father, He opens up fully and says, "Now they have known that all things which You have given Me are from You" (17:7, NKJV).

Summary

- Jesus was and is the Master Pray-er.

- He is also the Master Prayer Meeting Builder.

- Jesus only built one Church—a praying Church.

- God can refuse nothing to a praying congregation.

- Just watch what God will do with that little prayer meeting.

- Revival in the Church is as near as our prayer meetings.

- The Upper Room was no accident. It was in the heart and mission of Christ the moment He called His disciples to come and follow Him.

- The Holy Spirit is not given randomly. He comes to the local church. To the local *praying* church.

- We are to pray for and expect revival to take place in each of our local churches.

- Christ alone is the completely vertical Person. He did everything by prayer.

Mentoring Group Discussion

1. Today discuss each of the above summary statements.
2. Walk through the Gospel of Luke, marking "P" in the margin wherever you catch Jesus and His disciples in prayer. And mark "HS" wherever you find the Holy Spirit. (You will often note a connection between the two.)

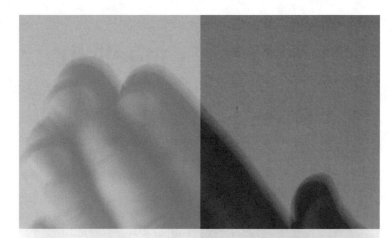

CHAPTER FIVE

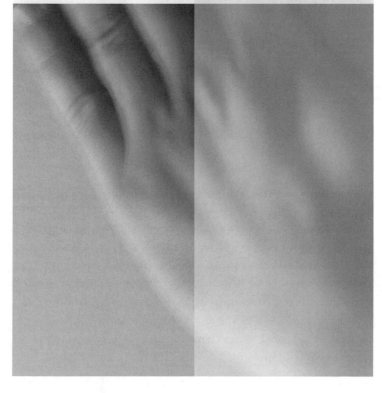

Prayer and Evangelism

If ever there was an "apostle of prayer," it was Armin. As you know, it was Armin's pastors' prayer gathering in Los Angeles that invited young Billy Graham to hold a crusade in 1948 . . . and the rest is history.

—David Bryant, Founder and President,
Concerts of Prayer International;
Director of National Prayer Committee

Armins' passion for prayer has had a profound effect on my life. His drive to motivate people to pray for revival has had a major influence on my passion to pray for spiritual hunger in myself and in the church. We need another Armin to be raised up in this decade!

—Jonathan Graf, Editor,
Pray! Magazine

"Prayer evangelism" has become a modern-day buzz word. It includes everything from prayer walking, prayer journeys, neighborhood houses of prayer, prayer triplets, prayer mapping and more. As remarkable as it may seem, Armin Gesswein wrote his graduate school thesis on prayer evangelism in the 1920s. Needless to say, he was a few steps ahead of his time.

Our chronic tendency is to dichotomize prayer and evangelism. It seems more often than not that we emphasize one to the exclusion of the other. Some are more up-reach, others more out-reach. Armin shows us that this inclination is contrary to the New Testament paradigm and contrary to an authentic Christian lifestyle.

When we read, "The Lord added to the church daily those who were being saved" (Acts 2:47, NKJV), we are reading about a consistent lifestyle of evangelism that proceeded from a consistent lifestyle of a praying congregation. We are not reading about a special evangelistic meeting; in fact, nowhere do we read, "They devoted themselves to evangelism." Many times, however, we read, "They devoted themselves to prayer" (see Acts 1:14, 2:42, 6:4; Romans 12:12; Colossians 4:2). For them, both prayer and evangelism were a lifestyle and the one flowed naturally out of the other.

> Bill Bright, one of the greatest evangelists of all time, said, "Don't be surprised if you hear one day that I have given myself to a ministry of intercession."
> —Armin Gesswein

To illustrate this principle Armin reached back in history to the revival in which he participated in Oslo, Norway.

> In 1937 and '38 I took part in the Norway revivals, where we found God working in churches and prayer-houses all over that lovely land. One of the strongest awakenings took place in a downtown Oslo church, where the prayer meetings had been dead. Scarcely anyone had been attending. The pastor had become so discouraged that he was about to discontinue altogether.
>
> Then something happened—first in his own heart and life, then in his praying and preaching, and finally in the other public services of the church. It was not long until a great outpouring of the Holy Spirit came to that local

church in an abundant flow that quickly influenced the other neighboring churches as well. Soon the entire city felt the impact. It started with prayer and flowed out in evangelism. That is the essence of prayer-evangelism.

The New Testament pattern of evangelism is embodied in the Church. Evangelism is rarely personal evangelism; rather it becomes church evangelism—churches bringing forth converts, even producing and reproducing other churches. Praying, Spirit-filled churches become the standard and the standard-bearers of the gospel. The risen Lord Jesus Christ gave the Great Commission and at once built His new Church for fulfilling it.

Evangelism also becomes revival-evangelism and gives us the biblical basis for New Testament revival. Peter became an evangelist, able to wield a two-edged sword bringing revival to the Church and deep conviction of sin to the unchurched. Peter the pray-er became Peter the revivalist, as well as Peter the evangelist. There is little doubt as we begin the twenty-first century that on the whole the evangelical churches of America are not lacking in methods of evangelism, but in results. Could the critical issue be the missing link of revival-prayer?

> ## The devil fights prayer because he knows it's the only thing that fights him.
> ### —Armin Gesswein

Armin saw Jesus as the Master Revivalist and the Master Evangelist. He would often say, "If we do what He tells us to do, He will do what He says He will do. God's Word is very plain regarding the coming of the Holy Spirit: He 'gives the Holy Spirit to those who obey Him' " (see Acts 5:32).

More than once Armin reminded me, "Fred, to be an evangelist requires the same gifts as a revivalist—both call people to life. An evangelist calls people to life who have yet to be born again while a revivalist calls people to life who have already been born again."

Despite our misguided efforts which have polarized evangelism and prayer, Acts 1:8 permanently solidifies them in one indissoluble union. Jonathan Edwards brought this same emphasis in his classic treatise *An Humble Attempt to Promote Explicit Agreement and Visible Union of God's People in Extraordinary Prayer for the Revival of Religion and the Advancement of Christ's Kingdom on Earth*. The "revival of religion" is what happens in the Church when God sovereignly pours out His Holy Spirit on the local congregation. And "the advancement of Christ's kingdom on earth" refers to the evangelism of lost souls in the world. Both work together when God's Spirit is flowing.

Pearl Goode

The story of Pearl Goode must be told in connection with Billy Graham's ministry. It reveals the true revival-prayer secret. It dramatically demonstrates the connection between prayer and evangelism.

If every work of God can be traced to some kneeling form, the praying of Pearl Goode, a widow from Pasadena, California, is most telling. She was one of the few great intercessors I have known. Her life radiated Christ and her heart pulsed with the Spirit of prayer and praise. Hidden away in her apartment close to Fuller Seminary, she prayed to her Father in secret and He rewarded her openly (see Matthew 6:6).

When Pearl Goode prayed in our meetings we at once felt the divine lift. Heaven and earth got together in a hurry. Driving her to one of our revival conferences was a

rare privilege. In the car she told me how the Holy Spirit
laid two major burdens heavily on her heart for intercession. One was for Billy Graham and his crusades, and the
other was for our conferences for revival and for the
preachers. When in her eighties, she would tell of the
powerful preachers in her day, such as Seth Rees, and
how the holy awe and power of God would rest on the
people in his meetings.

I was deeply moved as she told how God gave her a
special call to intercede for Billy Graham, and that she
would spend whole nights in prayer just for him and his
new ministry. The Holy Spirit constrained her. She just
had to do it. At once I was reminded of the Norway revivals, when the leaders prayed each morning, "Lord, bless
my intercessors today!"

At first Billy Graham did not know of Pearl Goode and
her God-given intercession. In fact, he did not know how
vast an amount of praying God was raising up on behalf
of his ministry. It was no doubt an answer to his own
praying as well, for I know of no other evangelist in our
time who has made such a strong effort to get people to
pray for him.

After hearing about Pearl and learning that she was a
poor widow, Billy made provision for her to attend his
crusades so that she could pray right at the scene of action. She would find a quiet room where she could give
herself to prayer and intercession.

Pearl lived to be nearly 90. She always made me think
of Anna in Jerusalem, "a widow of about fourscore and
four years, which departed not from the temple, but
served God with fastings and prayers night and day"
(Luke 2:37, KJV). Who knows how much of the New
Testament beginnings under John the Baptist and Jesus
can be traced to the kneeling form of Anna in the temple?

The time came when the Lord called Pearl home. My
wife and I attended her funeral in Pasadena. I did not see

any news reporters there, but the presence of the Lord was profound.

Present also was Mrs. Ruth Graham and some of Billy Graham's associates. Toward the close of the service Ruth stood up beside the open casket to speak briefly. Her face seemed to reflect the light from heaven as she pointed to the body of Pearl Goode and said: "Here lie the mortal remains of much of the secret of Bill's ministry." Those words will not be forgotten! This secret of intercession is almost lost in our churches today. It is not surprising that God "wondered that there was no intercessor" (Isaiah 59:16, KJV).

Summary

- Prayer and evangelism are inseparable.

- Prayer evangelism is good; revival evangelism is better.

- Jesus is the Master Evangelist and the Master Revivalist.

- Acts 1:8 permanently links revival-prayer with evangelism.

Mentoring Group Discussion

1. What is meant by prayer evangelism?
2. Why are these words inseparable?
3. What is the difference between personal evangelism and church evangelism?
4. What do the evangelist and the revivalist share in common?
5. What can we learn from the case study of Pearl Goode?

Left: the Gesswein family, 1920s. Armin is on the right, standing.

Below: Armin beginning his ministry as pastor of a Lutheran church, Long Island, N.Y.

Armin as a student, 1920s.

Armin and Reidun,
early in their marriage.

Reidun, 1937.

Early Gesswein family photo.

Armin (right) aboard ship with a colleague during the Norway revival of the 1930s, most likely traveling between speaking engagements.

Armin and Rev. Frank Poole at prayer tent during Bremerton, Washington crusade, 1950.

Armin in the late 1950s
or early 1960s.

Later in his life, golf
was a favorite pastime
for Armin.

Armin speaking during the 1990s.

Reidun joined Armin occasionally to speak at prayer events.

Armin and Reidun's
fiftieth wedding
anniversary.

Armin and Reidun with some of the grandchildren, 1998.

Armin preaching.

Armin with Billy Graham—a long-time friend and coworker.

An after-dinner message.

Armin in 2000. He remained active in ministry until his death in 2001.

CHAPTER SIX

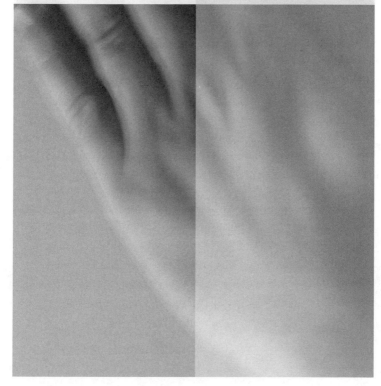

Praying the Promises of God

Of the many Christian leaders I have known and worked with, none has influenced my life more than Armin Gesswein, who was a friend, mentor and father-in-the-Lord. Reflecting on the four decades of friendship and interaction (often on a daily basis as Armin officed in our building), I am reminded that it was his life which most spoke to my heart. Always an optimist, always believing that God not only "can" but "will," and always catching a moment to say, "Let's pray together about this!" Armin seemed to have a direct line to the Throne Room. May his mantle fall upon many in this next century!

—Harold J. Sala, Founder and President,
Guidelines International Ministries.

Tarry at a promise, and God will meet you there.

—D.L. Moody

The Bible is the asking book and the answer book. We should never pray without reading the Bible and never read the Bible without praying.

—Armin Gesswein

I am frequently asked to write a book on prayer but I simply say, "It's already been written—the book of Acts."

—Armin Gesswein

Armin Gesswein did not pray in tongues. Without a sense of inferiority, he freely recognized that many of his friends had the gift and that God certainly still gives the gift. He seemed to enjoy, however, describing the Bible as "the inspired prayer language for every believer."

There is nothing like speaking to God in His native language. Nothing gets God's attention faster than when He hears His Word quoted, particularly when quoted by an expectant soul.

Like Armin, his early mentor, Uncle Am, lived to be ninety-three years of age. It was at his haystack prayer meeting (see Chapter 2) that Uncle Ambrose Whaley taught the young, impressionable Armin a principle that would change his life: "Young man, learn to plead the promises of God!"

Armin accurately referred to the promises of God as "the molds into which we pour our prayers." He explained that they foretell what to expect. They shape our praying. They motivate, direct and determine our supplication. Pleading the promises of God makes Christian praying distinct. In a very real sense, we as Christians pray from the answer to the answer. That's what faith really is. We take God literally at His Word. What He says He will do, we trust Him to do. And we trust Him to do it. What He tells us to do, we do, trusting it will be best for us. And we obey Him.

> ## Young man, learn to plead the promises of God!
> —Ambrose Whaley

This mentality takes Bible reading to a higher level. While it is certainly God's voice to us, it also becomes the platform from which we can give expression back to Him. He promises; we believe. We act on His Word by believing what He has said. In this sense, every prayer that reaches the throne of God starts there.

One of the cardinal doctrines of the Christian faith is prevenient grace. Simply stated, this is the notion that we seek God only because He sought us first. This being the case, we must never lose sight of the fact that true prayer starts with God.

This reality is further reinforced by the doctrine of human depravity and original sin. No one seeks after God (Romans 3). Therefore anyone who has a desire to seek God has already experienced the activity of God, who has placed that desire within them.

Prayer is something that does not come naturally to any of us. We do not know how to pray as we ought, so the Holy Spirit intercedes for us with groans too deep for words (Romans 8:26). We are encouraged to "pray in the Spirit" (Ephesians 6:18) which means to pray at the impulse and under the control of the Holy Spirit. It should come as no surprise that since the Bible is referred to as "the sword of the Spirit" (6:17), the words of the Bible are a primary tool or platform by which the Holy Spirit initiates prayer.

> Call to me and I will answer you and tell you great and unsearchable things you do not know. (Jeremiah 33:3)

> If you believe, you will receive whatever you ask for in prayer. (Matthew 21:22)

> You may ask me for anything in my name, and I will do it. (John 14:14)

In a very real sense we pray for the answer with the answer in mind. This is the way our Lord prayed. His Father promised; He believed; He acted on His Father's Word. Remember how your elementary school math book had all the answers in the back? Perhaps you were one of those rare students who first worked out the problem and then looked up

the answer. Some of us, however, looked to the back of the
book for the answer and then, with the answer in mind, we
worked out the problem to match it.

> Prayer needs three organs of the body
> that are all located on the head. The
> ear hears His word to us, the tongue
> repeats what we've heard from
> Him back to Him, and the eye
> looks expectantly for the answer.
> —Armin Gesswein

In a sense, this is how we pray. We pray with God's answer in view and expect it to be fulfilled. As with a math
book, there are different answers for different problems and
different methods of obtaining the same answer. So the Bible
contains thousands of promises which hold the answers to
thousands of our daily needs. The Bible becomes not only
our prayer book, but our answer book as well.

On a practical basis how does this work? How do we find a
promise that fits our need? Fortunately the promises of God
are life-sized, big enough to meet every need we face. We can
lay aside horoscopes; all we need is God's Holy Word.

When we lack joy, Philippians is where we need to read
and pray. When we're suffering and stressed, we want to
read and pray our way through First and Second Peter.
When it's encouragement we need, Second Corinthians is
where we read and pray. For revival we read and pray Acts 1
and 2, as well as Revelation 1-3; for evangelism, we turn to
Psalm 2 or Matthew 10.

In response to a challenge from Armin, I decided one year
to read through the Bible, marking an "R" in the margin ev-

ery time I found something that looked, smelled or tasted like revival. Over one thousand R's later, I marked my final "R" next to the phrase, "Even so, come, Lord Jesus" (Revelation 22:20, KJV). The coming of Christ is what revival is all about and when He bodily returns the second time, all our prayers for revival will reach their final fulfillment.

> ## You can't hang your hat on one verse.
> ### —Armin Gesswein

It has been said that as Protestants we don't have a prayer book. Wrong! Our prayer book is the Bible; we just need to learn how to put it to good use. Less than a year before his death, Armin wrote the following letter to his ministry friends:

> The Bible is our one real Prayer Book. The best way to pray is to pray the Scriptures. That means we plead the promises and pray God's language. We pray God's own Word back to Him. This inspires faith and without faith, prayer goes nowhere; nothing happens. It is not biblical. It is not really Christian praying. God followed up on all of this in me, and suddenly was urging me to once again pray through the book of Acts. [He was ninety-three years of age at this time and he was still learning to pray through the book of Acts! Lord, have mercy on the rest of us!]
>
> God slowly, surely, let the words hit me in prayer. I get on my knees. I wait on the Lord. I have been urging ministers to disciple their leaders and churches to pray for revival by praying through the book of Acts. It is still the greatest book on revival ever written. My prayer is for God to enlarge our steps and quicken our pace toward revival. According to your Word, make us book-of-Acts Christians, and make our churches book-of-

Acts churches. Make us strong in prayer, and in the power of the Holy Spirit.

Even the plain things of Scripture must be revealed to us by the Holy Spirit.
—Armin Gesswein

We all need new challenges in prayer, especially when it comes to praying for revival. All too often our revival-praying is too general. The book of Acts, on the other hand, keeps us focused and makes revival very specific and tangible.

Albert Barnes, in his famous *Barnes' Notes on Acts*, writes,

> This book [of Acts] shows that revivals of religion are to be expected in the church. . . . If by means of revivals the Holy Spirit chose at first to bless the preaching of the truth, the same thing is to be expected still. If in this way the Gospel was at first spread among the nations, then we are to infer that this will be the mode in which it will finally spread and triumph in the world.[1]

Praying Through

Elijah knew how to "pray through." He went up on the top of Mt. Carmel, put his face to the ground, and the seventh time he asked, he saw a cloud the size of a man's hand and he instantly knew the answer was in the bag. Too many of us stop praying the sixth time we ask. We stop too soon and often fail to see the great things God had in store.

Revival-praying goes something like this: Nothing, nothing, nothing, nothing, nothing, nothing. Then, everything! For Elijah it was the rain. For us, the rain is God's Holy Spirit. The early church did not pray for four or five days. They prayed for ten days clear through until they received the promise of the

Father, the mighty downpour of God's Holy Spirit. That is Upper Room prayer—praying until we receive.

The 1930 Revival of Bethlehem, Norway

One day Rev. Thorleif Holm-Glad, assistant pastor and leading evangelist in Bethlehem, Norway, was walking through the empty sanctuary when the caretaker stopped him with the announcement, "See these empty seats? This year there will be revival in this church." Holm-Glad was startled! He was well aware of the many empty seats in their church services. But he also knew the caretaker: a very humble, soft-spoken man, never a platform man or public speaker. He was just a quiet person, doing his job well— and, a man of prayer.

"This year there will be a revival in this church." Holm-Glad was also a musician and a composer. Those words wanted to sing in him, but could they really be true?

Yes, they were true. It happened just as the caretaker had spoken. That very year the revival broke out in the Bethlehem congregation—and what a revival it was! It seemed to never stop. It changed the whole congregation and brought revival to other churches throughout Norway. It turned out to be one of the greatest revivals of this century. On and on the meetings went as the fire of passion for God kept burning for about nine years. In the Bethlehem congregation alone, thousands repented and were converted to Christ. Like the infamous northern lights, the revival lit up the land of Norway.

The next year after the caretaker had spoken these words, in the middle of the ongoing revival, the congregation had a festival, celebrating the outbreak of the Awakening. Once again the caretaker came to Holm-Glad. "Do you remember a year ago when I told you there would be revival in this church that year?"

"How could I forget it?" Holm-Glad replied.

"Now," said the caretaker, "the Lord allows me to tell you something I was not free to tell you at that time."

He took Holm-Glad up into the pulpit. Standing there together, he said, "If you knew how often, while cleaning this church, I knelt behind this pulpit. I shed many tears, praying God to send the Holy Spirit in revival power to this church! And then I received. I sensed a breakthrough. God gave me the assurance that revival was on the way. It was only a matter of time."

Holm-Glad had a very tender heart, and wept many tears as he would tell this story in his local church and in other neighboring congregations throughout Norway.[2]

Armin often told me that in 1931 he made Jeremiah 33:3 his life verse: "Call unto me, and I will answer thee, and show thee great and mighty things, which thou knowest not" (KJV). He saw that revival was in fact God's "great and mighty work." Since he wanted God's best as his ministry, he pursued it with all he was worth and prayed it persistently throughout his life. Armin enjoyed telling how Dr. Charles Fuller also claimed Jeremiah 33:3 as his personal life verse.

The boldness and tenacity with which Armin grabbed the promises of God is clearly seen in his April 1992 prayer letter to ministry friends in which he spoke about the seven golden prayer promises in the Gospels.

- Whatever you ask in My name, that I will do, that the Father may be glorified in the Son. (John 14:13, NKJV)

- If you ask anything in My name, I will do it. (14:14, NKJV)

- If you abide in Me, and My words abide in you, you will ask what you desire, and it shall be done for you. (15:7, NKJV)

- In that day . . . most assuredly, I say to you, whatever you ask the Father in My name He will give you. (16:23, NKJV)

- Whatever you ask the Father in My name He may give you. (15:16, NKJV)

- Until now you have asked nothing in My name. Ask, and you will receive, that your joy may be full [complete]. (16:24, NKJV)

- In that day you will ask in My name. (16:26, NKJV)

He wrote in the prayer letter,

When I was a boy, my father once gave me a five-dollar gold piece. I felt rich! I treasured it, and kept it for the right time before I used it. Here Jesus gives His disciples and us seven gold pieces: freshly minted prayer promises; golden nuggets. Who can estimate their value? When the Lord offers the same thing seven times we had better listen.

Can you imagine what would happen in the gold rush days if suddenly they saw not one, but *seven* large nuggets of pure gold? Imagine them lying right out on the surface of the ground, before their very eyes, not in some stream or mountain. What a rush that would trigger! A mad scramble would follow. If someone captured even one of the seven, he would feel rich—full of joy. His long wagon-wheel trek over the Rockies would have been worth it all.

But here in full view are seven golden nuggets in God's Word. Any one of us can have all seven without interference or competition. Cash in on them! We can ask for and receive anything in Jesus' name—He said so. This is Jesus' invitation for us to share in truly great praying. If we are willing, we are able to pray as He prayed and to get answers like His. All we need to do is to pray the Word of God—to dare to plead the promises. The disciples went for this gold. They lived on these riches the rest of their lives.

> You can't get a thousand-dollar
> answer for a ten-cent prayer.
> —Armin Gesswein

One day, for example, Peter and John went to the temple to pray. A paraplegic sat begging for money. Peter's mind instantly flashed to the riches he had in Christ. "Silver and gold, I have none," he admitted, "but what I have I give you. In the name of Jesus Christ of Nazareth get up and walk." And at once the cripple jumped to his feet and proceeded to run, skip and dance around the courtyard, giving praise to God. A whole new wave of revival followed. It was all part of the gold. Peter learned to receive by pleading the promises of God (see Acts 3).

Let's be smart. Let's wake up to prayer, repent of prayerlessness, learn to pray and go for the gold. Learn to pray to God in the language He best understands.

Summary

- The Bible is our prayer book.
- The Bible is the heavenly prayer language for every believer.
- There is nothing like talking to God in His native language.

- The promises of God are the molds into which we pour our prayers.

- Pleading the promises of God makes Christian praying distinct.

- Every prayer that reaches the throne started there.

- There has never been a natural-born pray-er.

- Praying in the Spirit is when we pray Scripture, using the Bible, the sword of the Spirit.

- When we plead the promises, we are praying with the answer in view.

Mentoring Group Discussion

1. What does it mean for the Bible to be our prayer book?
2. Why does Armin Gesswein call the Bible "our heavenly prayer language"?
3. What does it mean to plead the promises of God?
4. What prayer promises are you pleading?
5. What revival promises are you pleading?

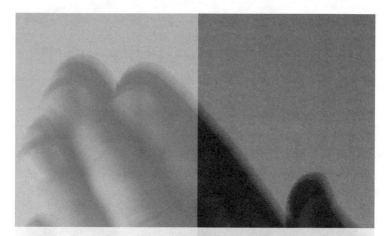

CHAPTER SEVEN

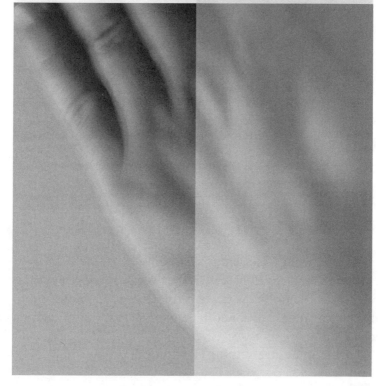

Prayer and the Holy Spirit

My dear friend Armin and I shared the same vision
with passion, for Christlikeness to come to the Church
worldwide and that an unprecedented spiritual awakening come to the lost for the glory of the Lord Jesus. I
miss him greatly. This veteran revivalist was always as
fresh and as real as a morning sunrise.

—Joy Dawson

If the Holy Spirit doesn't do it, there's nothing to it.

—Armin Gesswein

To be full of the Holy Spirit is to be full of prayer; and to
be full of prayer is to be full of the Holy Spirit.

—Armin Gesswein

Without pre-Pentecostal prayer, there would be no
Pentecostal power.

—Armin Gesswein

Armin Gesswein's final book, *How Can I Be Filled
with the Holy Spirit?*, received glowing praise from
many quarters. "Armin Gesswein knows more
about spiritual revival and has taken part in more revivals
than any living person," Sherwood Wirt said. "This book
promises to be an enduring classic." Bill Bright added, "For

the seeker this book will open the door to the most exciting life imaginable." And Stephen Olford commented, "Every pastor and lay leader should read this book. . . . It will bless them and their ministry."

> There is no such thing as Holy Spirit
> power without Holy Spirit prayer.
> —Armin Gesswein

In the preface to the book, Armin testified to his own experience with the Holy Spirit:

> Early in my life, I spent seven months seeking to be filled with the Holy Spirit. I searched Scripture and soon found that there is what can be called a twofold Christian life: *born* of the Spirit and *filled* with the Spirit.
>
> This quickly turned into a double search. I searched the Greek roots of the New Testament and *God* searched my roots. And my roots were not Greek; they went all the way back to Adam.
>
> My search took me to many kinds of meetings and altars of prayer—sometimes all night, sometimes half-nights. During these months God taught me many things. He also alerted me to many dangers, especially the danger of seeking manifestations of the Holy Spirit.
>
> Did God answer my prayer to be filled? Yes, He did—wonderfully—just perfect for me. He also gave me certain manifestations—gifts—sovereignly suited for my life and purpose and ministry (1 Corinthians 12). You, too, may be having certain struggles concerning the work of the Holy Spirit, so I'll share some of my own, with the prayer that you may find help and clarity in your search. I'm eager to share a fresh discovery which greatly clarifies and simplifies the experience of how to be filled with the Holy Spirit. The exciting thing

is that it is found in such plain Scripture. The wonder is
that we could miss seeing it.[1]

Armin's teaching on the Holy Spirit is predominantly from
John's Gospel. He says that while many scholars recognize
John's Christology as unsurpassed, they fail to see that his
pneumatology (his teaching on the Holy Spirit) is likewise second to none. John's Gospel begins by showing how the
shekinah glory of God—His manifest presence, which rested
over the tabernacle of Moses and miraculously led God's people for forty years as a cloudy pillar by day and a pillar of fire by
night—now rests on Jesus. John writes: "The Word was made
flesh, and dwelt among us, (and we beheld his glory, the glory
as of the only begotten of the Father,) full of grace and truth"
(John 1:14, KJV). All through the Gospel of John we behold
the glory of God in Christ. John shows that this same glory is
also imparted to us by His Holy Spirit. In John 17 Jesus prays,
"And the glory which You [Father] gave Me I have given
them" (17:22, NKJV).

Armin taught that the structure of John's Gospel reflects
the two streams of theology, both of Christ and of the Holy
Spirit. The first part of John (chapters 1-12) teaches about
our eternal life in Christ. The second part (chapters 13-16)
teaches about how Christ lives out His life in us by the filling
of the Holy Spirit. John takes us to the Upper Room where
Jesus tells us about the Holy Spirit whom they should know
and whom they were yet to receive. Then he tells us just
how, when and where the Spirit was to be received. Right
there, in the same Upper Room where they meet intimately
with Jesus Himself, they were soon to receive the Holy
Spirit.

John's use of the word *receive* is an interesting case in point.
Our first need is to become Christians, and John at once tells

us how. "As many as received Him, to them He gave the right [power, authority] to become children of God" (1:12, NKJV). Later, the same word, *receive*, is used in reference to the Holy Spirit: "Receive the Holy Spirit" (20:22, NKJV). Both uses of receive quite obviously refer to two distinct experiences.

I'm not a fanatic on healing; I just believe in it.

—Armin Gesswein

We are not urged in Scripture to receive "the baptism" or "the experience of sanctification" or even "the indwelling" or "the power," but the *Person* of the Holy Spirit. He then empowers, sanctifies, fills, gives gifts and graces and does all kinds of new things in us and through us. Instead of seeking experiences, we seek and receive Him. With John as our teacher, we are led to receive Christ, and then we are led to receive the Holy Spirit. He too is a Person to be received definitely, just as we received Christ and became a Christian.

Armin would say, "John's message and method, which He got directly from Jesus Himself and which helped to bring about a unified Christianity in the first century, is just as greatly needed today." Armin was careful to avoid both controversy and compromise. When he tackled difficult subjects he always tackled them graciously. Though Armin Gesswein never spoke in tongues, he loved to talk about the gift of tongues in order to guard against "charismaphobia." His teaching sought to strike a biblical balance:

> Tongues are indeed prominent in the New Testament churches, but never dominant. They never are allowed to take control. They need to be kept under control. Many gifted believers learn this the hard way. And if they are not humble and teachable here, they have more prob-

lems. I know many who have a genuine gift of tongues; but they have learned to obey God's Word and learned about His controls. The result is they not only continue in the church "endeavoring to keep the unity of the Spirit in the bond of peace" (Ephesians 4:3, KJV), but have become strong intercessors helping to bring revival and strong witnessing power to the congregation.

> When you're revived, you go through
> thick and thin without thinning out.
> —Armin Gesswein

Armin's Own Journey

Listen carefully to Armin describe his own journey into Holy Spirit fullness:

I had to get information on the fullness and power of the Holy Spirit from plain Scripture. That took time. I did not know much about the Holy Spirit early in my ministry. I did not mix with groups that professed to know much about the Holy Spirit. As Lutherans, we were separatist, but we were very strong for Scripture as the inspired Word of God.

I began to meet some who claimed to be filled with the Spirit, and that quickened my pursuit. But I was also greatly disturbed, because some of those who claimed to be Spirit-filled fought against others who made the same claim. I couldn't figure this out. But instead of letting it throw me, it made me search all the more for answers. There was almost a constant feud between those of the Pentecostal tradition and those of the holiness movement. The one group stressed the signs and wonders and the others stressed sanctification and holiness. I was stretched. God was working me over! It took time. It still takes time.

The price for the gift of the Spirit is the same for us as it was for those who received it in the New Testament. There are no bargains or get-rich-quick schemes with God. God had to work me over and chisel me down to size. The Lord, I learned, does not dump the Spirit on an unprepared vessel.

Many churches proclaim Christian truth and assume that their hearers are all Christians. They do not lead their people into personal faith in Christ and to the assurance of eternal life. This leads to presumption, false hope, false peace and false comfort. This is very serious. It is not the way of the Word of God. The same thing is happening when it comes to the Spirit-filled message. The New Testament does not assume or presume here. It is as clear about our need for finding and living the Spirit-filled life in Christ as it is for finding Christ and knowing for sure that one is a Christian. I have learned that signs and wonders, as well as sanctification, are available to us. We don't need to dichotomize. We can harmonize.

I was greatly convicted of my need, both of power and of sanctification. In fact, at one time I thought of quitting the ministry because I saw that the Lord did not send His disciples out into further ministry until they were "endued with power from on high" (Luke 24:49, KJV). But quickly the Lord got to me with this word: "He gives the Holy Spirit to those who *obey Him*" (see Acts 5:32). That was a great help. So I pursued the way of obedience.

Hindsight is a great teacher. In my search, and in His searching me, I see that I got into some self-effort and legalism. I was mixed up. For a while I would leave the manifestations and the way He wanted to fill me all up to God, but in reality I was seeking the manifestations themselves. When I put fillings and feelings ahead of faith, I put the cart before the horse. In this case, the cart was full of fascination and even ecstatic feelings. But there was no horse!

It took me a while to find out the dangers of seeking manifestations. I well remember my hunger when I would read testimonies like Charles Finney's. Like when he described his baptism in such flood-tide language ("waves and waves of liquid love flooded my being, so that I literally bellowed forth the unutterable gushings of my heart" . . . and even spoke of asking the Lord to stop or he would die). I quickly got down on my knees and prayed: "Lord, that's what I want!" But nothing happened. There were no waves. Not even a ripple! Later I learned that the Scripture does not speak of hunger in that way. It speaks of hungering and thirsting after *righteousness*, and that such would be *filled* (Matthew 5:6).

I also read of D.L. Moody, who received a mighty baptism of the Spirit. We know that after it he was different and became the greatest evangelist of his time, moving two continents closer to Christ. He freely called this experience his "baptism in the Holy Spirit." All this stirred me deeply. Again I got down on my knees and prayed: "Lord, that's what I want." I was willing to call it the baptism or any other term in Scripture. But again, nothing happened! Nothing!

Often I was discouraged and confused. At times I prayed with some who claimed high-powered experiences because they were considered strong and very reputable leaders. All the time I kept on studying God's Word and read the experiences I considered reliable. I did not merely want to play it safe. I wanted no nonsense, no error. I wanted to give no room for the devil. For me it has to be biblical. Main scripture and plain scripture. I needed to avoid going off into the deep end. One important leader said, "If the devil can't hold you back, he will try to shove you into fanaticism and make you useless." That rang true to me.

Mixing with all schools of thought in my search was good, because I found out later that the Lord wanted to use me with any and every group and denomination. I agree with D.L. Moody, who said if he thought he had any sectarian blood in him, he would ask God to drain it before nighttime!

One night I attended an all-night prayer meeting in Brooklyn. The leading minister in charge came to me as I was kneeling with many others. He laid hands on me and urged me to just let myself go. To let myself go blank. That alarmed me and very much surprised me that this man whom I held in high esteem would engage in that kind of a method. I said nothing out loud, but to myself I said, *That's wrong. I'll not do anything like that. God never says to do that in His Word. It is dangerous and even spiritualistic. It leaves room for a wrong spirit or spirits. It is not the way of the Holy Spirit.* In any case, nothing happened.

I've seen the real gift of tongues, and it is wonderful. But I've seen a lot that is not wonderful! It certainly is a field where Satan does a lot of counterfeiting. God is not the author of confusion. And we don't have to get into false experiences and then later test them to find out if they are genuine. If, on the other hand, you do speak in tongues, by all means have it tested and proven according to Scripture.

Christ Himself is not only our Savior, but our example and role model in this great matter of being filled with the Spirit.
—Armin Gesswein

Armin provided seven questions. They are straightforward and simple. They are most helpful for anyone who seeks to be filled with the Holy Spirit. They are neither emotional nor intellectual and are useful while coaching virtually any sincere seeker. They are plain and simple conscience questions, and they take us at once to the taproot of our being. They have everything to do with being filled with the Spirit of God, who is holy.

1. Am I **truthful?**

This has everything to do with being filled with the Spirit because Jesus is the Truth, and the Holy Spirit is the Spirit of Truth. Anyone who is to be filled with the Spirit must be a truthful person. Specifically, are there any conditions under which I tell a lie? Would I ever tell a little lie? God cannot lie, and He will not motivate us to try to do it for Him. Satan, on the other hand, is a liar and the father of lies. Any kind of lying must be dealt with, confessed and repented of. Do I stretch the truth? Do I exaggerate? In court we are asked to "tell the truth, the whole truth and nothing but the truth." Jesus holds court in us every day, and that is exactly what our real Judge asks of us in order to fill us with His Spirit. He is the Spirit of Truth and when we are filled and controlled by the Holy Spirit we will also tell the truth, the whole truth and nothing but the truth.

2. Am I **honest?**

This is a similar question, though it moves beyond our words to deal with our motives. Am I a person of integrity? Does my manner of life speak truth to people? Do I ring true? Am I authentic? Some people appear highly spiritual and they only want to talk about spiritual things. This is often a smoke screen. People who can't talk about life apart from spiritual things often have skeletons hiding in their closet. Can I be trusted with money? Have I stolen anything? "Let him who stole steal no longer" (Ephesians 4:28, NKJV). Yes, and let him also take back what he has stolen. Many revivals came about as people made restitution.

I'm talking about anything you've borrowed that you haven't given back—or forgot to pay back! The devil whispers, "Forget it; nobody will remember." But that old liar knows as well as you do that it was dishonest. There are at least three parties, and maybe four, who know all about it: the devil knows, the Lord knows and you know. And the party you borrowed from and didn't pay back most likely remembers it too—people usually have long memories when it comes to money!

Quoting a friend, Armin said, "Lord, don't let me do anything I'll have to confess if a revival comes." The filling of the Holy Spirit is revival. To be filled we must face, confess and repent of anything in our life that is not 100 percent honest before the Lord.

A Case Study
by Armin Gesswein

The Holy Spirit broke through in a local congregation in which I was ministering. One elder, a dear man who taught the adult Sunday school class and was heavily involved in the work of the church, had borrowed $1,000—$500 from an old preacher and $500 from another person—so he could go to Florida and invest it in what he thought was a good real estate deal. He went there and lost it all. Some time later he returned, got busy in his church again, but forgot about the $1,000 he lost. He again resumed his leadership there and also taught Sunday school.

There was much prayer. I preached there for many weeks. We were expecting revival, but there was a hindrance, a block. The atmosphere was negative. We were earnestly asking the Lord to show us what the hindrance was. Then I began to hear about this leading el-

der. People knew about his Florida venture but had not
talked about it. I was really surprised, for he was a good
man and a real leader.

It was a Saturday. I said to the pastor, "We must go to
see him—today."

He was surprised to see us—and even more surprised
when I confronted him with the Florida deal. I felt very
tender and sympathetic toward the man. He began to
weep and said, "But I don't have the money!" I replied,
"Dear brother, it really does not depend on whether you
have the money. If you would but take your weary legs
to both of these parties, ask for forgiveness and simply
give each of them $5 every time you get a paycheck, in
that way you would at least start to pay back the money.
You are a leading elder in this church and you need to
do what is right before God." He cried. The pastor cried
and I cried.

"Pray for me," he said. "I'll have to face the whole
congregation with this." Sunday came, and so did the
revival! He sat just a few rows from the front with his
wife. Suddenly, before I got up to preach, he arose. Immediately we all sensed a divine Presence in the service.
Tearfully he confessed his sin before the whole congregation and asked forgiveness.

It was like pulling a plug, and the Holy Spirit began to
flow! Others at once stood up, asking for forgiveness for
things they had said and done. On and on it went, both
at the altar and among people in the congregation.
What a melting time as the heavens opened up. The revival broke through. We did not get out of the church
until the afternoon. The Holy Spirit answered prayer.
He started by orchestrating honesty and repentance.
That's how he brings us into the fullness of the Holy
Spirit.

3. Am I **prayerful?**

Jesus was very, very prayerful. Particularly prior to His baptism, when the Holy Spirit came upon Him, He was in the act of praying. As we have seen, prayer saturated His life (see Chapter 4). This is primary—foundational. There is no record in Scripture of anyone who was filled with the Spirit who was not a prayerful person. There is no record of anyone *continuing* to live as a Spirit-filled person who does not *continue* to be a very prayerful person.

4. Am I **obedient?**

While this principle appears throughout the Bible, Acts 5:32 explicitly says, "The Holy Spirit, whom God has given to those who obey him." To be filled with the Holy Spirit is to be under the control of the Holy Spirit and to be empowered by the Holy Spirit. It is only logical to assume that the Holy Spirit will be motivating and empowering us to obey God. At the same time, He will be enabling us to supernaturally overcome sin.

Conscience is the taproot of our being—there is nothing deeper in a man. The Holy Spirit leads us to clear our conscience and get right with God and man. This repentance, brokenness and restitution is not emotionalism. It is the activity of the living God and His Holy Spirit.

The revival we need will bring conviction of sin and repentance and get us into the depths of biblical holiness. Sanctification will not take the place of power but will make it truly biblical.

5. Am I **pure?**

Everything the Holy Spirit does is holy. The moment He fills us, He begins the work of making us holy, like Himself. Jesus said, "Blessed are the pure in heart: for they shall see God" (Matthew 5:8, KJV).

Am I pure in my relations with the opposite sex? With my own sex? If we are to be clean we must come clean. The Holy Spirit does not fill unclean vessels. He cleanses them with Christ's precious blood so that He can fill them. A familiar Bible verse states, "If we confess our sins, he is faithful and just to forgive us our sins, and to cleanse us from all unrighteousness" (1 John 1:9, KJV). It is easy to buy into the part that talks about forgiveness, but it's not enough to say, "Lord, *forgive* me." We must also say, "Lord, *cleanse* me." If we pray for cleansing, we do not need to keep on living in the same sin and uncleanness. When we pray to be cleansed from all unrighteousness, then He is ready to fill us. God does not fill an unclean vessel.

> There is no such thing as Holy Spirit
> power without Holy Spirit prayer.
> —Armin Gesswein

6. Am I **easily offended?**

This question quickly reveals the self-life, which is often the last to go. It too must be dealt with. When Christ was crucified, our self-life was crucified with Him.

We must deal with our inclination to point fingers at, be critical of or gossip about those who have offended us. The Holy Spirit, using His Holy Word, will help us deal with a whole brood of wrong attitudes which are called sin. As we search the Scripture so the Scripture searches us.

7. **What am I living for?**

This is really the big question; it hits at the core of our lives—our motivation. It is impossible at one and the same moment to live for Christ and to live for self. No one can serve two masters. The Holy Spirit's *modus operandi* is to exalt Christ, to enthrone Christ, to bring us into conformity with

Christ. His constant effort, therefore, is to call us to whole-hearted, white-hot devotion to Christ. My dedication to God must be full and complete. The chief end of man is to glorify God and to enjoy Him forever. We are here to live the Christ-life and to this end we must be filled with His Holy Spirit, even as *He Himself was filled to live that life.*

Armin Gesswein's Story

I was preaching in special evangelistic services in a Baptist church in New York City, not far from the Manhattan Bridge. Many had been praying for revival. I had for months been prayerfully seeking to be filled with the Spirit. I wanted to get the matter of the Holy Spirit settled in my own life and was so burdened about it that I had little desire to pray about anything else. I withdrew from the others and quietly prayed to the Lord to clear this all up for me and settle it. I sensed the Lord Himself drawing near. He questioned me, "You are a Christian?" There was no audible voice, and yet I knew it was Him.

"Yes, Lord."

"How did you get saved?" God asked me.

"Lord, it was by faith. Like Luther, I had a struggle for years, but it was by faith."

"Now what is it you want?"

"Lord, I want to be filled with the Holy Spirit from the innermost to the uttermost."

"Is there any other way than by faith? Don't you know that 'without faith it is impossible to please God' (Hebrews 11:6)?"

It all came together for me right there and then! I saw that I had been seeking manifestations and experiences. Experiences like those I heard about and read about. At once I prayed, "Lord, I'm done praying. Right now I *take the Holy Spirit to fill me* from the innermost to the uttermost. And I don't care if I ever have a wave or a ripple. It's settled right now by faith."

It was near midnight. I excused myself and left the prayer meeting to walk to my room. I was not married then and was staying in a guest room . . . near the front of the building. Suddenly, as I was leaving the prayer room, I began to feel as if I was wrapped in a cloud of glory! It was a manifestation of the Spirit. And I had never read about one like this in Finney's or Moody's or anyone else's experience. It was His manifest presence, right there as I walked on into my room. Then when I got to my room and soon into bed, the same glorious presence of the Holy Spirit pervaded and filled my being for hours, manifesting Himself in different ways in my body as I worshiped and praised the Lord, full of His love and joy and faith and peace and assurance. What a wonderful night of answered prayer in my life!

When I'm asked, "What all happened in your room that night?" I usually say the reason I don't tell all of that is that you might do what I did. You might get your eyes on manifestations and seek an experience like that. It would hinder you. The point is: When did God fill me with the Spirit? Was it when I knew His glory and had those manifestations that night? No! It was in that prayer room I actively received the Person of the Holy Spirit and knew it was settled, feelings or no feelings. Prayer got me into the Spirit-filled life, and the Spirit-filled life got me into prayer in a new and much enlarged way.

I early saw prayer as the greatest secret in the Christian life and ministry. I saw that if I am to learn the way of revival I must learn to pray and somehow develop a strong prayer life. Nothing is more important. Now the Holy Spirit enlarged it and also made the Bible come alive as never before, making it my supreme prayer book. I should tell you that I began to have a new and very real faith in my life, trusting the Lord for everything, including my finances. I began to know and experience a wonderful guidance in every way. And isn't that one of the real results? Was it not so even with Jesus? And doesn't Paul say that "as many as are led by the Spirit of God, these are sons of God"? (see Romans 8:14). Full control and complete guidance. These are major marks of the Spirit-filled life. It has, by His grace, been a wonderful life; as my wife Reidun says, "It's getting gooder and gooder."

If the Holy Spirit doesn't do it, there's nothing to it.
—Armin Gesswein

Having read Armin's story, it is equally refreshing to read Reidun's story of how she too was filled with the Holy Spirit not long after they were married. She had been converted to Christ in Oslo, Norway, where she was studying to become a nurse. You can feel the authenticity of her experience as she shares in humility and vulnerability:

My life and desires changed when I received Jesus into my heart as my Savior. I wanted to be like Him. I longed to please Him. As I studied His Word and became acquainted with His ways, a deeper longing for the Holy Spirit to be a reality in my life was growing. Daily I would take time to read His Word and pray, and I began to pray that I might be filled with the Holy Spirit. This went on for some months, and the Lord showed me my own lack of full consecration.

When Jesus reached me that night and became my Savior, I thought nothing would ever take His peace away from me. However, when I prayed now, He showed me that I was not full of the Holy Spirit. So of-

ten I wanted my own way. I often wept as I prayed as He
revealed things in my life that grieved Him. I longed to
be a vessel for His use. Then He convicted me of past
sins which I had never confessed and needed to face and
repent of.

One, for example, had to do with honesty. Years ago,
as a girl, I had stolen some money and never confessed
it to my school teacher who was involved in it. What
made it doubly hard for me to confess was that she was
not a Christian. I tried to forget it, but the Lord let me
have no peace. I could not wiggle out of it. So I commit-
ted it all to Him, asked His forgiveness at the same time
that I wrote to this teacher. In my letter I asked for her
forgiveness and also sent money, with interest, making
restitution.

A remarkable thing happened. This teacher never answered me—for six years. And then I got news that she
had died. But on her deathbed a minister led her to faith
in Christ. She was not able to speak, but the Lord reminded her of my letter. So she wrote a note to me that
all was forgiven and we would meet in heaven someday.
What a lesson! I learned how living faith came along the
line of my obedience. Faith and obedience—what a
wonderful pair! So one night I drove down a stake and
told the Lord I believed Him right then to fill me with
His Spirit. And He did! By faith I was filled.

That day I started a new chapter in my spiritual journey and began to learn new, precious lessons in prayer
and intercession and a deeper and closer walk with the
Lord. I am still learning. I saw Jesus in a new way, so
precious and wonderful! The Holy Spirit came and glorified Jesus and continues to do so after these many
years.

While Armin and Reidun Gesswein sought to mentor Christian leaders into the Upper Room, their goal was not the Upper Room, but the outpouring of the Holy Spirit which comes to the Upper Room. And it was never intended to end there. Out of that Upper Room, Christ reaches a lost world through a revived Church.

Summary

- As we seek the fullness of the Holy Spirit, the Holy Spirit searches us.

- John the Apostle had a keen Christology and an equally keen pneumatology.

- The first half of John's Gospel teaches us to have eternal life in Christ and the second half to have the fullness of the Holy Spirit.

- The Person of the Holy Spirit comes to give us power for holy living and for fruitful service.

- It is wrong to seek an experience; it is not wrong to seek the Lord.

- Tongues are prominent but never dominant.

- Seven simple, straightforward questions to prepare us to be filled:
  a. Am I truthful?
  b. Am I honest?
  c. Am I prayerful?
  d. Am I obedient?
  e. Am I pure?
  f. Am I easily offended?
  g. What am I living for?

- The primary ministry of the Holy Spirit is to exalt Christ. The Holy Spirit first makes Christ known to us, then He makes Christ known through us.

Mentoring Group Discussion

1. What does it mean to you to be filled with the Holy Spirit?
2. Respond to Armin's statement, "There is no such thing as Holy Spirit power without Holy Spirit prayer."
3. In what way does the Holy Spirit search us as we search for His fullness?

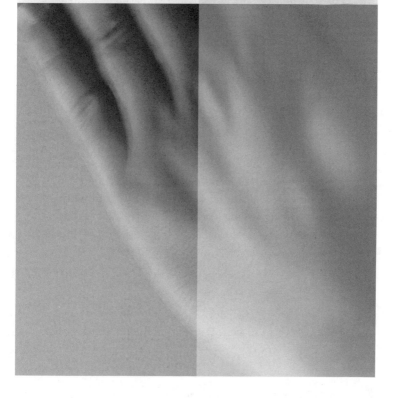

CHAPTER EIGHT

Prayer and the Church

An older man once told me, "The way you speak about revival reminds me a lot of Armin Gesswein." His comment made my day. For decades Armin was a gift of God to the Church and for decades to come his writings will challenge all those whose hearts yearn for another seaon of revival in the Church.

—David Mains

The Church was not born while someone was preaching, but while someone was praying.

—Jim Cymbala

The book of Revelation is the final call to revival for the Church.

—Armin Gesswein

The condition of the church may be very accurately gauged by its prayer meetings. So is the prayer meeting a grace-ometer, and from it we may judge of the amount of divine working among a people. If God be near a church, it must pray. And if He be not there, one of the first tokens of His absence will be a slothfulness in prayer!

—Charles Haddon Spurgeon

God likes to see His people shut up to this, that there is no hope but in prayer. Herein lies the Church's power against the world.

—Andrew Bonar, 1853

Armin Gesswein began his ministry as a local church pastor, and though he became a seminary professor, evangelist, revivalist, author, mentor and leader in the modern prayer movement, his heart never left the local church.

In 1990, when Armin Gesswein was asked to write a brief history of the fiftieth anniversary of Minister's Prayer Fellowship and Revival Prayer Fellowship, he was asked the question, "What lessons have you learned over the fifty years of prayer revival ministry?" He mentioned a couple of golden secrets which cut to the heart of his revival-prayer theology of the church:

> Make no mistake about it—the primary venue for revival in the New Testament is the local church. The Holy Spirit's greatest works are done through the church, and the pastors are the keys to the local church. The first church, the Upper Room in Jerusalem, reveals God's golden secret for all genuine revival and spiritual awakening.

We build walls. God doesn't build walls; God digs deeper wells.
—Armin Gesswein

Beyond the Gospels and the Book of Acts, Armin loved the first three chapters of the Book of Revelation. He saw that they formed God's last and loudest call to revival in the Bible. In these chapters, the seven local churches are receiving a fresh revelation of the risen Christ. And isn't that—a fresh revelation of the risen Christ—the starting point of revival? Each of the seven churches are then called to return to Christ, to return to their first love, to repent, to come into obedience and to overcome. Armin taught that each church has the opportunity to step into revival, with Christ standing with His feet perched on the threshold, knocking on each church door, appealing to each one who has ears to hear what the Spirit is saying to them.

> We as Americans lead the world in
> many things, but we do not
> lead the world in prayer.
> —Armin Gesswein

I have file folders full of handwritten and hand-typed notes from Armin, exhorting me to invest my life in the local church: "Fred, we must get prayer into our churches." And he often added with a gentle goad, "And how is revival-praying in your local church, Fred?" At other times he would write, "Fred, we must build praying pastors who can build praying churches." And again, "Fred, I'm praying for your congregation. . . . You are on the way, but I'm praying for you to see it through all the way into the Upper Room."

Armin loved the big events. He attended each of the Billy Graham Lusanne Conferences for World Evangelism. He attended prayer conferences in Seoul, Korea. He and I sat together at the Promise Keepers Clergy Conference on the floor of the Georgia Dome in Atlanta. He insisted, however, that until prayer take hold of individual local congregations, the prayer movement would remain superficial at best.

The New Testament prayer meeting and the New Testament Church were synonymous terms. Armin lived with a driving passion to see local churches take this biblical reality and make it a twenty-first-century reality. To show that he was not only a theologian, but also a practitioner, consider his five specific recommendations for each local church:

1. The Prayer Meeting

Every local church and their pastor needs to give priority to their prayer meeting, regardless of what day of the week it is scheduled. There is nothing sacred about Wednesday night. "If you want to see how popular the church is, attend Sunday morning worship. If you want to see how popular the pastor is, attend Sunday evening. If you want to see how popular God is, attend the prayer meeting," said Armin.

2. A Prayer Room

Each local church needs a room devoted to prayer, which becomes a training center and a focus of increased activity, including well-kept records, bulletin boards with answers to prayer, maps, missionary files and, if possible, internet access to interface with similar ministries.

3. A Prayer Coordinator

Their responsibility under the senior pastor is to give leadership to prayer ministry, prayer training and equipping. This prayer coordinator may choose to form a *prayer mobilization team*, similar to a missions committee, Christian education committee or hospitality committee.

4. A Prayer Conference

Just as many churches have missions conferences, they would do well to have prayer conferences. Whether three days in length or a full month, specialized focus throughout the year will raise the level of intercession in the congregation and build it into the lifestyle and culture of the people.

5. Prayer Training

Just as Jesus taught His disciples to pray, there needs to be a fully developed prayer training strategy in each local congregation. These five specific initiatives give tangible guidelines so that each local church could become a praying church and enter into the Upper Room.

Four Forms of New Testament Prayer

Armin taught that four forms of New Testament praying are modeled and mentored by Jesus Christ: (1) private praying; (2) prayer partners; (3) small-group praying; (4) church prayer gatherings. Every one of these forms is found in connection with the great revivals throughout the flow of church history.

The first, of course, takes place in the private prayer closet; others take place in the corporate setting. One must never separate these four, suggesting that one is superior to the other, or that one could be excluded on matters of personal preference. Any Christian who sincerely enters into one phase of prayer will readily become a part of the rest. Turning this around, if a Christian says he does not care for prayer meetings and would rather pray alone, a reality check usually reveals that such a person is not praying alone very much, either.

Jesus Christ is never working against Himself. The same Jesus who intends me to pray alone will also make it possible for me to pray corporately. And if I love Him and love meeting with Him in one form of prayer, I will love the other forms as well. Let's take a closer look:

1. Private Praying

Jesus taught, "But when you pray, go into your [most] private room, and, closing the door, pray to your Father, Who is in secret; and your Father, Who sees in secret, will reward you in the open" (Matthew 6:6, AMP).

This kind of closet prayer or solo prayer goes first—that's how Jesus did it. Whatever He taught about praying, He practiced. That is what gives His statements and promises about prayer a quality all their own. No one ever prayed like Jesus; He taught and modeled solo prayer.

His private prayer closet was most often on some mountain or hillside, out in the desert or beneath some olive tree. The key is not in the cloister of a room, but in the place of solitude and without distraction. It was on one such occasion a disciple requested, "Lord, teach us to pray" (Luke 11:1).

Revival usually begins with one praying Christian—and not necessarily a preacher. Any plain-vanilla Christian qualifies. Jesus promises, "Every one that asketh receiveth" (Luke 11:10, KJV). If the times got so bad that only one intercessor was left on earth, like Elijah, we could still have a revival. Living in days of declension and apostasy, it is encouraging to know that "The effectual fervent prayer of a righteous man availeth much" (James 5:16, KJV).

I never saw a revival with front pews empty.
—Armin Gesswein

Jesus' call to solitary prayer may lead some of us to reply, "My life is so hectic; where can I find solitude?" But if Jesus told you to go into your "most private room," you must have one somewhere; He never gives us an impossible assignment.

It is important to have this kind of special getaway place to pray; many never get into the holy habit of daily praying for this very reason. We read that Jesus "continued His habit of retiring to lonely spots and praying" (Luke 5:16, Williams). Jesus had them and He has them for us as well. Ask Him where He wants to meet with you for that spiritual, intimate, private time.

2. Prayer Partners

Jesus taught, "Again I say to you that if two of you agree on earth concerning anything that they ask, it shall be done for them by My Father in heaven" (Matthew 18:19, NKJV).

This is without doubt one of the most powerful prayer promises in the Word of God. The point, however, is not only in two people praying together, but in their complete agreement. The original Greek word is *somphaneo*, from which we get the word *symphony*. This kind of agreement is difficult; only the Lord can bring two people together like that. When the full story is told, this is invariably found to be part of the pattern of revival praying.

This promise to two or more people praying in agreement should be a great challenge and tremendous encouragement to Christian parents. Surely our Lord had parents in mind here—parents and best friends.

3. Group Prayer or Prayer Triplet

Jesus taught: "For wherever two or three are gathered (drawn together as My followers) in (into) My name, there am I in the midst of them" (Matthew 18:20, AMP).

Revival is both individual and corporate. God revives the individual, but never in isolation from the others. Revival usually starts with one praying Christian and then moves on to others who are like-minded. In all true prayer, no matter how large or small the group, this loving agreement is important; it is the heart of all revival. Revival-glory is manifested in such a fellowship. God's holy *shekinah* is always first revealed to those who are thus united in prayer in the innermost part of His holy temple.

In a sense the most significant trend of our times is the fresh emergence of many kinds of prayer fellowships, both in the local churches and in citywide gatherings. Something happens in those hours when you meet together on your knees before God. Christ says, "By this shall all men know that ye are my disciples, if ye have love one to another" (John 13:35, KJV). The prayer cell produces it, and the world notices it.

4. All-Church Prayer Gathering

Jesus commands it: "And, being assembled together with them, [He] commanded them . . . [to] wait for the promise of the Father. . . . These all continued with one accord in prayer and supplication, with the women, and Mary the mother of Jesus, and with his brethren" (Acts 1:4, 14, KJV).

Here Jesus brings prayer up to its highest capacity in all-congregation praying. When praying reaches this strength, we know we are on the eve of great revival. This is already happening in many communities. In the Upper Room in Jerusalem Jesus had for the first time in history gotten together about 120 members of the Church. Every one of them was a strong intercessor. This is an all-time high for the *Guinness Book of World Records*. There had never been so many in the same place on the same wavelength. Indeed, this was not the only miracle, but the highest and last great miracle of the Risen Christ on earth. To this hour, a great all-out prayer meeting in any congregation is still the highest miracle of Christ in any community. What is there on earth to compare with it? This is Christ's amazing pattern for the pathway to revival.

We have forgotten that when Christ built His Church, He built a prayer meeting. We have forgotten that there was not a single member of that Jerusalem congregation who was not in the prayer meeting. We have forgotten that the place where they counted their numbers was in the prayer meeting. We have forgotten that united prayer was its supreme method for everything—that everything was done by prayer. We have forgotten that prayer was the very organizing principle of that Church, of its new oneness and unity of its officers, of its victory in battle against every form of persecution and opposition.

From beginning to end, the book of Acts shows the intimate and unfailing connection between prayer and every work of God. If God did apart from prayer what He has promised to do in answer to prayer, the very point of prayer would break down. When God is about to do a work on the earth, He always starts by waking up His people and calling them back to prayer.

When prayer is on the increase—all four forms of praying—real revival is at hand. Armin also suggested that to motivate and activate the entire church by prayer, the following four steps should be employed:

1. *The pastor himself needs to develop prayer in his own life.* He is the center hub. He and his staff should meet with other area pastors and staffs in a prayer fellowship. The leadership of this group may be rotated so that everyone may share what they have received regarding prayer from Scripture. They can also share problems and pray for one another.

2. *The church staff and key leaders need to meet regularly for prayer under the leadership of their pastor (see 2 Timothy 2:2).* The pastor should use this time to develop and train these key people in their prayer life. Every one of them, whether they teach a Bible study, do visitation or lead worship, is a potential prayer leader. Prayer needs to permeate the church life and culture until it becomes "The way we do things around here," or more accurately, "The way God does things around here."

3. *Neighborhood Bible study and prayer group leaders should meet for prayer with the key leaders.* As often as possible, the pastor and staff should attend as well. Sunday school teachers should also be encouraged to join in, so they too can become prayer-builders and leaders in all they do.

4. *Every church member should be involved in a neighborhood prayer-fellowship group with trained leaders.* This kind of total church involvement is ambitious, but it can occur with the encouragement and commitment of the pastor and key leaders.

These small groups may take on a variety of flavors, but no matter what they study otherwise, they must include prayer—however simply at first. As the small-group prayer life grows, so will the love, life, power, outreach and growth of the entire church. This builds prayer into the total congregation, making it a praying church like the one in the book of Acts.

Devoted to Prayer

It felt good to sit down; I was exhausted. But it was a good exhausted. I was glad for the four-hour flight back from San Francisco to Atlanta. I had just completed facilitating a four-day prayer summit with Armin Gesswein at Simpson College in Reading, California. Dozens of pastors found spiritual refreshment. Countless college students confessed stubborn sins and received life-transforming freedom in Christ. Many Christian leaders said their lives would be permanently impacted. As I sat in seat 32-C cruising at 35,000 feet, I dropped the tray table, took out a pad of paper and drew a line down the middle. In the left-hand column I wrote "A Church that Prays." In the right-hand column I wrote "A Church Devoted to Prayer." It's the church devoted to prayer that truly becomes the Upper Room.

A Church that Prays	A Church Devoted to Prayer
1. Prays about what it does.	1. Does things by prayer.
2. Fits prayer in somewhere.	2. Gives priority to prayer.
3. Prays when there are problems.	3. Prays when there are opportunities.
4. Is able to fulfill its purpose by itself.	4. Is able to fulfill its purpose only by the grace of God.

5. Announces special times of prayer—some in the church show up.

5. Announces special times of prayer—the church shows up.

6. Asks God to bless what it's doing.

6. Asks God to enable them to do what He is blessing.

7. Is frustrated by financial shortfall—backs down from projects.

7. Is challenged to fast and pray through times of financial shortfall—receives money by faith and moves ahead with its projects.

8. Does things within its means.

8. Does things beyond its means.

9. Sees its members as its parish.

9. Sees the world as its parish.

10. Is involved in the work of man.

10. Is involved in the work of God.

Three days after my birthday in 1993 I received a hand-written note from Armin which oozed with passion for the local church.

> Dear Fred:
>
> We must pray believingly for a good prayer disciple-ship training plan. Must? Yes. It is His Great Commission (Matthew 28:19-20). And His mandates are mandates. Let's not forget—He will give us His full Upper Room pattern.
>
> The way I see discipling these days is that most of it stops at the cross, like most of Jesus' discipleship did then. Then they all scattered—forsook Him. After the resurrection Christ really was busy. He got them all together again (Acts 1:3) and gave them His new and full and final mandates. Jesus then moved them into the second and final stage of discipling and discipled them all the way into the Upper Room.

Then and there He began the real deal in the prayer
meeting. This quickly became His new Church. The
whole commission began at Pentecost. Since then the original Upper Room is the real pattern for everything. That must be our goal in all this
prayer mobilization. The Throne is a very busy place,
but there is always room for one more. I'd like to be
known at the Throne. Let's meet there often.

We must get revival into the churches now, along
with the increasing revival of prayer. We must also be
praying about prayer discipleship training in the
churches. All major athletes who are already pros insist
on coaching and training. How in the world can we in
the church minister in so major a matter as revival in a
minor manner? We need training.

Shake the love around.

May it be your best year.

Do you say Amen? God bless you every day.

Armin

When Armin went to Seoul, Korea, for the International
Prayer Assembly in June, 1984, it was as if he died and went to
heaven. He saw the manifestation of what he had been preaching for decades. It was as if the Church of Acts was being
replayed in the twentieth century. They didn't simply pray
about things; they did things by prayer. He noticed that the
Koreans "rose a great while before day" in order to pray and
would often pray through the night. They had prayer meetings
where thousands gathered. And answers? Miracles of all kinds.
They were taught to pray through until the answer came.

And their churches were growing by leaps and bounds.
He watched and reported,

They are not an aberration; they are not fanatics. They
are normal, New Testament Christians. My own vision

of revived praying [leading to] producing and reproducing churches was greatly renewed and reaffirmed. I
saw there what I have known from precious revivals,
and what is plainly shown in God's Word. This was indeed God's way in the great revivals of Norway.

Armin called us to get back to the biblical secret of prayer
and praying churches:

> We must learn again to wait on the Lord in prayer . . . to
> follow the tender, gracious, distinct leading of the Holy
> Spirit as we pray. [We must] learn the prayer method of
> getting things done on our knees. Prayer is the ministry
> out of which all other ministry is born: born of God—
> born, not made or manufactured. Prayer is where we
> work and where God works.

In one of his final prayer letters (February 2001), a little
more than a month before his death, he wrote the following
prayer letter to ministry friends.

> Dear Friends:
>   Reidun and I just returned from Atlanta where we held
> another module of our "College of Prayer" gathering,
> held in Lilburn C&MA church. Our fellowship was en-
> riched by the Lordship of Christ . . . in His discipleship . . .
> and in worship and prayer. Fred Hartley is the pastor of
> this growing congregation. He is also the chairman of our
> prayer mobilization team. They have a beautiful new
> sanctuary building, and the spirit of prayer and revival are
> more and more in evidence.
>   Our plan is to hold one module of our three annual
> modules there to "see it happen" in a church setting. Each
> time we invite some specialist to fit this vision into ours.
> This time it was Steve Hawthorne, who heads a growing
> "Prayer Walk" ministry. Many are the testimonies from
> such "walks," and the Lilburn church has also added it in

their effort to reach their community. Some 90 ministers and wives and church leaders attended this module. Many were first-timers. And quite a few different denominations were represented. And what gracious hospitality the Lilburn church and leaders gave us!

I spoke on "How to Build a Praying Congregation." And on Sunday morning in their chapel gathering on "The Great Commission is our Mission." Reidun also testified, telling of the revival in Oslo, Norway, where she became a Christian . . . and of the wonderful prayer testimonies of some who helped to pray that great revival into being. In the main sanctuary, Dr. Ivar Overgaard, pastor of the Salem Evangelical Free Church of Staten Island and also our main key man for Norway . . . spoke on "Why They Waited in Prayer Before Pentecost" (Acts 1). The Lord was very present, and there is a strong sense of the Holy Spirit at work there. Many lives are being transformed, marriages restored and some testified to wonderful healings. To God be the glory!

Shake the love around,

Armin

Summary

- God's only venue for revival is the local church.

- The first three chapters of the book of Revelation are God's final and loudest call for revival found anywhere in the Bible.

- The key to local church revival prayer ministry is the heart of the pastor.

- True New Testament discipleship takes us all the way into the Upper Room.

- Prayer is the ministry by which all true ministry is born.

- Reaching a lost world through a revived Church is the vision of the Upper Room.

Mentoring Group Discussion

1. In what way did Armin's view of the local church parallel his view of the universal need for revival?
2. From Armin's perspective, why was local church revival a necessity?
3. In what way did the Korean church model Armin's vision of the Upper Room?

CHAPTER NINE

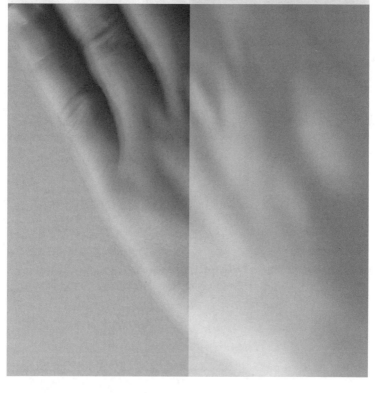

Prayer and the Sovereignty of God

Long before the great prayer movements of our day, Armin Gesswein was the movement! In the earliest years of my ministry, when I thought about the power of united prayer, the first name that came to my mind was Armin Gesswein. His was a voice crying out for years, even decades, into the wilderness of neglected prayer, and that voice bore fruit beyond measure. The thriving prayer movements of our day, I believe, can be traced to that lone, unwavering, passionate voice.

—Dick Eastman, International President,
Every Home for Christ

God will not do apart from prayer what He promises to do in answer to prayer.

—Armin Gesswein

Every work of God can be traced to a kneeling form.

—D.L. Moody

Revival cannot be organized, but we can set our sails to catch the wind from heaven when God chooses to blow upon His people once again.

—G. Campbell Morgan

Revival is that sovereign work of God in which He visits
His own people, restoring and releasing them into the
fullness of His blessing.

—Robert Coleman

One great doctrine of the Christian faith is the
sovereignty of God; one great practice of the
Christian faith is prayer. Tragically, evangelical
Christianity has allowed a great doctrine to unnecessarily
hinder a great practice. In the name of God's sovereignty,
many have argued against prayer by asking, "If God is going
to do what He wants to do anyway, why bother praying?"

In an essay published in March of 1992, Armin Gesswein
brilliantly removes us from the horns of this seeming di-
lemma to the delightful adventure of biblical prayer. Commenting on Philippians 4:13, "I can do all things through
Christ who strengthens [energizes] me" (NKJV), he writes,

> All the time people try to challenge me theologically on
> the matter of prayer, saying, "Armin, God is great. He is
> sovereign. He is God. So He can get around to do what-
> ever He wants whether we pray about it or not." I re-
> spond, "God will not do apart from prayer what He
> promises to do in answer to prayer, and it is my Christian
> responsibility to search the Scriptures and find out just
> what He promises to do by prayer." What a revelation! It
> changed my thinking. There I learned that He does every-
> thing by prayer. His prayer promises give us complete
> coverage.
>
> They appear to be without limit: "All things whatso-
> ever," "everyone who asks receives," "anything," "Men
> ought always to pray," "everything by prayer and suppli-
> cation," "pray without ceasing." And if God wants us to
> pray without ceasing, it is because He wants to answer

without ceasing! Wonderful! It all comes down to this: Prayer is not everything, but everything is by prayer. When Christ told us to pray, "Your will be done on earth as it is being done in heaven," He intended to work out His sovereign plan through His people. Rather than prayer violating the sovereignty of God, it works within and under the sovereignty of God. This understanding raises prayer to an all-time high. No one more clearly demonstrates this principle than Jesus Himself. Jesus walked into answers to prayer throughout His life.

Since we are not simply talking about prayer, but prayer that brings revival, Armin applies the same logic to revival-praying. Dr. Richard Loveless of Gordon-Conwell Theological Seminary, in his book *Dynamics of Spiritual Life*, draws a strong distinction between Jonathan Edwards' theology of revival and that of Charles Finney. Edwards, Loveless argues, taught a sovereignty of God in revival while Finney taught almost a sovereignty of man in revival.[1] Gesswein would disagree. The following essay, "Revival Praying and the Sovereignty of God," provides his rationale:

> I hear it quite often that revival depends on the sovereignty of God, and when He decides to send it, it will happen. That sounds pious, but it is not as pious nor as biblical as it sounds. My answer to this is quick: Tell me something which is not under the sovereignty of God.
>
> Early on in my journey, I used to shoot up petitions very earnestly, expressing all my wishes and desires and aspirations, and then leave it all up to God. In that way I would come to know if it was the will of God. That would settle that. The problem, however, was that I would keep on with my usual lifestyle and never grow in intimacy with Christ. Nor did I grow in godliness.
>
> There is a lot of that kind of praying for revival. It is not pious praying; it is not even biblical. Prayer is the

key to heaven, but faith unlocks the door. There must be faith. And faith comes by hearing and heeding the Word of God.

The Word of God takes us right to the throne of God where all of its mighty sovereign action takes place. The book of Revelation reveals the sovereignty of God reigning from the throne of God. The throne, however, is at the same time drenched in worship, praise, prayer, supplication and intercession. Revelation is a tremendous book about the sovereignty of God and at the same time a tremendous book about revival-prayer. What eye-opening lessons these are! These are some of the highest and holiest and hardest lessons for us to learn about authentic New Testament revival-praying and its relation to the sovereignty of God.

> We're called to do the work of God,
> but only God can do it. That's why we pray. We're
> called to do the impossible, but only
> God can do it. He's got us again.
> —Armin Gesswein

Certainly another case study in the indivisible union of God's sovereignty and man's praying is the incarnation of Christ. Christ was fully God and fully man. He was not sometimes acting as God and sometimes acting as man. Specifically, when He walked on water, He was not more God; when He cried, He was not more man. He was fully God and man at all times in a perfect indivisible union. Similarly, the Church is walking incarnationally in this world. When we obey God in the power of the Holy Spirit in any area of life, that step of obedience is fully the work of God and fully the work of man. Regardless of whether it is in prayer, social action, domestic

kindness, civil justice or cleaning our child's vomit off the car-
pet, when we love others in obedience to Christ and do an expression of our love for Him, it is at the same time fully His
doing and fully our doing. So it is with revival. It is wholly the
work of Christ and wholly the work of man.

When He was on earth Christ constantly preached about
the kingdom of God. In this way He shows us the sovereignty
of God in action. He demonstrated that the kingdom of God
was always prayer-action. He walked into each new scene and
mighty work not as a surprise, but in answer to His own great
previous praying. After dying for our sins and rising from the
grave the third day, He took His enormous prayer-life straight
to the Throne where He now spends all His time.

Armin was asked the question, "Can we expect to see revival in
our churches again?" His matter-of-fact answer was, "Yes! Where
else would it come? Revival can only come to the Church."

Albert Barnes, a contemporary of Charles G. Finney, experienced real revival. It was said the revivals under his ministry
were not like brushfires, but more like strong, long-burning
coal fires. In his *Notes on the New Testament*, he says that the
book of Acts is

> . . . an inspired account of the character of true revivals
> of religion. It records the first revival that occurred in
> the Christian church. The scene on the day of Pentecost
> was one of the most remarkable displays of divine
> power and mercy that the world has ever known. It is
> the true model of a revival of religion, and it is a demon-
> stration that such scenes as have characterized our own
> age [1800s] are strictly in accordance with the spirit of
> the New Testament.
>
> The human mind is prone to enthusiasm and fanati-
> cism; and men might be disposed to pervert the gospel
> to scenes of wildfire, disorder and tumult. . . . It is well,

therefore, that there should be some record to which the Church might always appeal as an infallible account of the proper effects of the gospel, some inspired standard to which might be brought all excitements on the subject of religion. If they are in accordance with the first triumphs of the gospel, they are genuine; if not, they are false.[2]

Oh, to be known at the throne.
—Armin Gesswein

Barnes goes on to say,

This book shows that revivals of religion are to be expected in the Church. If they existed in the best and purest days of Christianity, they are to be expected now. If, by means of revivals, the Holy Spirit chose at first to bless the preaching of the truth, the same thing is to be expected now. If in this way the gospel was at first spread among the nations, then we are to infer that this will be the mode in which it will finally spread and triumph in the world.[3]

The revival in Norway which Armin tasted in his twenties was always seen by him as normal Christianity. Church growth in Norway did not succeed because of great promotional schemes or high-pressure methods. One looked in vain for spectacular or sensational ads in the papers. Instead reports of social transformation often became front-page headlines. The revival took hold of the church and profoundly influenced the lifestyle of the people. It was not a gradual revival, which simmers slowly until it is gradually felt by others; it was more like a tidal wave, sweeping through towns and bringing sudden, deep, dramatic change. There were no church splits; as in the case of the Jerusalem congregation in Acts, God Himself mended and wove the churches together into a continuous accord. Christians were winsome; many were won to Christ because of the believers' good conduct. "And the Lord added to their number daily those who were being saved" (Acts 2:47).

All types of people were converted to Christ. Both within and outside of the public services, people came under conviction of sin. People of all ages and classes became so conscious of their sin that they could not sleep at night. People were afraid to live—and even more afraid to die! Sometimes they would get up in the middle of the night and call a Christian friend or relative for advice. Some would walk six or seven miles to find someone to pray for them and help them find pardon for their sin and peace for their guilty consciences.

People who had not attended church for years would come to the meetings, drawn there by the Spirit. It was in this wild-fire context where Armin observed the reality and phenomenon of revival that few others in our generation have observed. He witnessed people who fought and resisted the reviving work of the Holy Spirit, and on the other hand, he witnessed people who embraced the reviving work of the Holy Spirit. He observed the synthetic wall we erect between God's sovereignty and man's responsibility virtually disappear. Some of the mystique of revival that blurs our thinking did not blur his.

The book of Revelation unfolds the judgments of God, and that is precisely what revival is: sudden and radical accountability—judgment beginning at the house of God (see 1 Peter 4:17). There is great joy in a revived church, and at the same time great judgment. The awe of God rests on the congregation. Revival brings a church to Judgment Day honesty. Conviction of sin strikes home, and repentance reaches the level of the conscience. As the country preacher said, "Don't do anything you will have to confess when revival comes."

There is only one throne and God is on it.

—Armin Gesswein

"Many say they are waiting for the last trumpet call for the second coming of Christ." Armin said, "Their problem is they are not hearing this first loud trumpet for the coming of the Holy Spirit to wake up our Church." While this trumpet blasts, Jesus is all ablaze—on fire from head to foot. His eyes are as a flame of fire as He walks in the midst of these churches with His feet also on fire as if they were burning in a furnace. And what is He doing?

There is only one throne and Satan is not on it.

—Armin Gesswein

Jesus is conducting this revival. And He is at work in all churches. In fact, He is conducting seven revivals at the same time. They are all a part of a divine circuit of churches. As these seven churches form a circle, so the Holy Spirit is often a "circuit rider" of sorts between churches. One church, like a lampstand on fire, can light up a whole city or community. That light can radiate, helping other churches to be revived.

Yes, God is sovereign over revival, just as He is sovereign over all things. He sovereignly invites us to step into it. We are not Muslims who stand at arm's length from their god, issuing a distant phrase: "if Allah wills." We are Christians who have an intimate love relationship with the sovereign God. His sovereignty does not give us an excuse to stand at arm's length from Him and wait for a future manifestation of His fiery holy presence—quite the contrary! We rise up and draw near to embrace Him and receive now the refreshing, renewing, revival Presence He has for us—not only every Christian, but every church. What are we waiting for?

Summary

- Tragically, evangelical Christianity has allowed one of its greatest doctrines (the sovereignty of God) to unnecessarily hinder one of the greatest practices (prayer).

- God will not do apart from prayer what He has promised to do in answer to prayer.

- Jesus walked into answers to prayer throughout His life.

- Tell me something that is not under the sovereignty of God.

- The book of Revelation is a great book of revival and a great book on the sovereignty of God.

- The incarnational life of Christ vividly demonstrates the indissoluble union between the sovereignty of God and the prayers of man.

- The Church is to walk in the same incarnational union.

- Revival praying draws us into the spiritual intimacy God desires for each of us.

Mentoring Group Discussion

1. Does there need to be a conflict between the two distinct doctrines of the sovereignty of God and the prayer of faith?
2. Why was Armin so fond of the book of Revelation?
3. Define revival.
4. Define revival-prayer.
5. What effect would it have on our faith to unite the doctrines of the sovereignty of God with the doctrine of prayer?

CHAPTER TEN

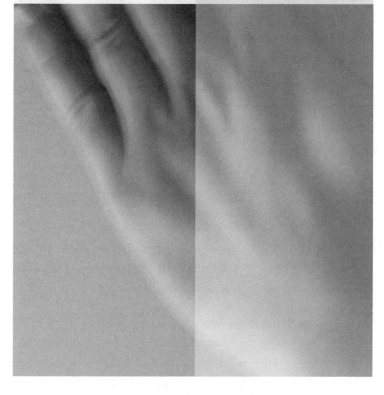

Prayer and the Inner Life

There was a refreshing beauty of authentic holiness about Armin Gesswein. He was for real, "an Israelite in whom there was no guile." Prayer and the promises of God's Word pervaded everything he did. Out of this atmosphere of faith came an anointed vision and burden for revival that was contagious. Persons close to him could not help but feel the love that radiated from his servant heart. Some of that love overflowed on me, and as with so many others, I will be forever grateful for the impact of his ministry upon my life.

—Robert E. Coleman, Professor of Evangelism,
Gordon-Conwell Theological Seminary

I have never known God to use a discouraged person.

—D.L. Moody

Always give preference to the spirit of contrition.

—Armin Gesswein

Armin was in his element. Having generously helped himself to the salad bar, he was now seated at a table with five or six pastor buddies, a group to which I was privileged to belong. Conversation was loud and animated. Armin was informally instructing us on everything from his healthy dietary patterns to his next trip to Norway.

"Eat living things," he smiled. "God tells me, 'Armin, eat living things. They are better for you.' So every day I have at least fresh fruit and fresh salads for two meals. I have to be careful; I can't eat as much as I used to."

Seeing the first lag in conversation, I jumped in. "Armin, do you ever get discouraged?" His eyes immediately looked up from his romaine lettuce. His mouth and countenance smiled. "I mean, as I pray for revival," I continued, "I get discouraged. It's almost like I can feel the weight of discouragement holding my prayers against the floorboards."

He reached his hand across the table, stuck out two fingers and enthusiastically said, "Two R's! When it comes to discouragement there are two R's. Recognize it and refuse it." From the tone of confidence in Armin's voice, I could tell I had struck oil. Rich, dark oil. Over the next forty-five minutes Armin took me and my pastor buddies to school on this entire matter of discouragement, which is certainly common not only to pastors, but to all pray-ers.

If you think this issue has little to do with revival-prayer, allow me to object. Successfully dealing with discouragement has everything to do with revival-prayer. In fact, as we shall see, God never uses a discouraged vessel. He doesn't use a discouraged preacher, a discouraged parent, not even a discouraged pastor. And I have been, at one time or another, all of the above. At that infamous salad bar luncheon with Armin, God used this principle of truth to set me free.

Like all practical theology, it starts with a proper understanding of God Himself—in this case, the God of all encouragement. The primary text is Second Corinthians 1:3-4: "Praise be to the God and Father of our Lord Jesus Christ, the Father of compassion and the God of all comfort, who comforts us in all our troubles, so that we can comfort those in any trouble with the comfort we ourselves have received from God." The phrase "God of all comfort" is translated from the Greek word *parakaleo*, which means "to call alongside, to encourage, to stand next to, to comfort or counsel." From this we can easily establish the principle that since God is the God of all encouragement, then everything He says and does is encouraging.

We Christians can go one better than that line from the old song "Home on the Range": "Where seldom is heard a discouraging word." We can say that from Christ there is *never* heard a discouraging word! This means that if discouraging thought patterns elbow their obnoxious way into our ministry, our prayer life or our family relationships, we can be sure of one thing: They did not originate with God.

Where, then, does discouragement come from? Some would certainly try to pin it on the devil—a "demon of discouragement." But although demons may foster unbelief and compound our theological errors, it is safer, at least initially, to place the blame for our discouragement at the feet of our indwelling sin nature. We are told, "anything that does not proceed from faith is sin" (see Romans 14:23). Certainly, we can confirm that discouragement is part of the unbelief pattern.

Again Armin stuck his bony finger across the lunch table. "Not only is discouragement a sin," he added, "it is one of the strangest, strongest, subtlest and sneakiest of sins. It is a strangler and it has a giant effect. It is hard to get hold of. It sneaks up on you when you aren't looking. We are told, 'all wrongdoing is sin' " (1 John 5:17).

Once we had established that discouragement is a sin that feeds on unbelief and self-pity, it became much easier to deal with. This is where Armin's two R's become helpful; while distinct from each other, the two go hand in hand.

First, we quit denying its existence—we recognize it, own it, acknowledge it. We call it what it is: the sin of discouragement, the product of unbelief and self-pity. Then we immediately proceed to the second R: We refuse it. It is intolerable. It didn't come from God—in fact, it is an utter hindrance to the Spirit of God. As D.L. Moody said, "I have never known God to use a discouraged person." No, discouragement will not send us to hell. But it doesn't help us lay hold of heaven either. It is one of those "sins that so easily entangle" (see Hebrews 12:1).

Since revival-prayer often resembles Elijah's rain-inducing prayer—nothing, nothing, nothing, nothing, nothing, nothing, everything!—discouragement can become a critical issue, keeping us from taking hold of everything. Like a boat hitting a sandbar, our prayer lives can quickly be trapped by the spirit of discouragement. To move forward, we need to soberly and honestly recognize and renounce the spirit of discouragement.

Discouragement is a form of self-life—it feeds off self-pity, self-indulgence, self-sensitivity, self-pampering. It is one of those secret indulgences of self-love to which we are all prone. We all enjoy withdrawing into ourselves and crying on our own shoulders for a while.

For me, discouragement was so prevalent in my life that it became sort of an alter ego. It was like a friend, albeit a lousy friend; for better or worse, it was my companion. I had no problem recognizing it; I had serious problems, however, refusing it. It was like having to amputate a gangrenous appendage: my discouragement smelled bad, looked bad and was bad, but it had been part of my life for so long that it took me a while to accept that it needed to be removed.

I began to realize how tightly and intricately its tentacles had woven themselves around my spirit. There was hardly an area of my life that was unaffected. Like a fog that silently slips in during the night, my spirit of discouragement had silently slipped into my heart and put my prayer life on the run. It was as if I couldn't take off and get airborne. I can't begin to count how many sermons I have preached, parenting lectures I've given my children and prayer services I've attempted to promote—all out of a spirit of discouragement.

I can vividly remember the afternoon in my study when I slipped to my knees and prayed a simple prayer, then opened my eyes and vividly, unequivocally renounced the spirit of discouragement. It was a watershed moment in my spiritual formation. The words Armin spoke into my life had taken hold. I can confidently and most gratefully say that I have been a categorically different person ever since. My praying is different—and so is my pastoring, preaching, parenting, promoting. And no more pouting! Praise the Lord! The discouragement was never from God in the first place, so once I recognized it for what it was—a product of my sinful self-life—disposing of it was a piece of cake.

Frankly, there have been several times over the past eight years when the spirit of discouragement rolled back in like a fog. Once again, however, I had the distinct pleasure of recognizing it and refusing it.

A few months after kneeling in my study and declaring treason on this alien spirit of discouragement with which I had previously cultivated quite a relationship, I found myself seated in a small hotel conference room in metro Atlanta with a dozen Christian leaders listening to David Bryant wax eloquently about his own story of "being converted to hope." As he quoted Romans 15:13, "May the God of hope fill you with all joy and peace as you trust in him, so that you may overflow with hope by the power of the Holy Spirit," I was like a sponge, absorbing spiritual truths as rapidly as they were being spoken. For me it was, in fact, a crisis conversion—a filling, a baptism and saturation of hope. Having exhaled the toxic spirit of discouragement, I suddenly realized the vital necessity of breathing in the life-giving spirit of hope. He is never discouraging nor is He ever hopeless. In these days of enormous challenge, we as Christ's servants need a fresh baptism of holy hope. Simply renouncing discouragement is only a half solution. Being converted to hope is the second half. It completes the work so that we can face the issue of ministry both in prayer and in daily experience. The future belongs to the hopeful. Any generation will run to the voice that gives it the most hope. By God's grace, let's be that voice.

Inspection or Introspection

Another piece of highly practical coaching Armin frequently gave is the subtle distinction between inspection and introspection. Any hungry soul with an ounce of desire to please God has felt the despairing effects of morbid introspection. Scavenging through the catacombs of our inner lives in an effort to rid our hearts of hidden lusts, vanity, selfishness and unbelief is depressing at best. On the other hand, the Scriptures call us to some sort of self-reflection by such verses as these:

A man ought to examine himself. . . . (1 Corinthians 11:28)

Search me, O God, and know my heart;
    test me and know my anxious thoughts.
See if there is any offensive way in me,
    and lead me in the way everlasting. (Psalm 139:23-24)

How can a young man or woman deal with moral purity issues without plunging headlong into unhealthy navel-gazing?

Conviction and repentance are always present in genuine prayer-revival. Armin and I have been with countless students, pastors and lay people who freely and openly confess their sins before God and man. In this context Armin felt right at home. It looked, smelled and tasted like the Norwegian revival in the '20s and '30s. He would often say, "Always give preference to the spirit of contrition."

In other words, when people begin to speak much of repentance and confession of sin from a broken, contrite heart, that is God, so *stay there*. Don't sing; don't pray about other things; don't dismiss for lunch; don't worry about the clock. Time stands still when God brings repentance. After all, that is the jewel God is looking for. It is the sacrifice acceptable to Him (Psalm 51:17). When we consider all God does to bring a person to the place of genuine repentance, we quickly understand why we give preference to the spirit of contrition.

In this context Armin would frequently coach participants toward healthy inspection and away from morbid introspection:

> Morbid introspection is always lethal. Any of us can find sin within. It is always bleak, dark and dismal when we subjectively look within ourselves. Like picking lint out of our navels, it is usually superficial at best.
>
> Inspection, on the other hand, is the exact opposite. God calls us to look away from ourselves in order to see ourselves. We look into Christ and into the objective mirror of His Word in order to see ourselves. . . . No one can see his own face without looking away from himself; as he looks away to an objective mirror, he can see what he actually looks like.

Similarly, God alone gives us an accurate view of ourselves only as we look to Him. And when He shows us ourselves, it is not only accurate, it is deep. He deals with core, motivational issues which are of primary influence and importance.

Christ the Sanctifier

At the core of his being, Armin was a Christ-centered soul. He himself was solidly grounded in Christ and he dynamically led others to rock-solid devotion to Christ. While Armin was an incessant troubadour of prayer, he never induced an unhealthy guilt nor a works-righteousness mindset. He never promoted a treadmill prayer regimen. The reason he not only preached revival-prayer but led people into revival-prayer was because he lived the Christ-life. He was a prayer-dependent, Spirit-led man.

We would often begin prayer summits not knowing where Armin was—and more practically, when he was likely to show up! As the facilitator, it often caused more than a little anxiety in me to know that within thirty minutes I would be expecting Armin to exhort the group. Time after time, Armin would remarkably show up at the precise moment his input was needed. I often joked, "Armin is like the Holy Spirit; he is rarely early but never late. Always just on time!" And he was.

Like a professional golfer, Armin never held the club too tight. His prayer leadership was always strong, but never forced. His teaching was commanding, but never belligerent. His coaching was directive, but never overbearing. His prayers were powerful, at times prophetic, but certainly never lacking humility.

The underlying reason for his grace and power was clearly found outside himself and fully found in the Person of the Holy Spirit. He knew the Holy Spirit and followed His lead. He taught in the Spirit, prayed and walked in the Spirit. He made a good glove and the Holy Spirit a good hand. He was so deeply broken, contrite, yielded and compliant that there was little left in Armin that hindered the free flow of God's Spirit or distracted from the glory of Christ. As a worthy mentor, for many of us he was "Exhibit A" of a Spirit-filled, Spirit-controlled man whose inner life was permeated by revival-prayer.

Summary

- When it comes to discouragement, there are two R's: recognize it and refuse it.

- Successfully dealing with discouragement has everything to do with revival-prayer.

- God is, after all, the God of all encouragement.

- Discouragement is not normally a demon. It is a sin that feeds off unbelief and self-pity.

- Discouragement will not send us to hell, but it sure doesn't help us lay hold of heaven.

- After we renounce the spirit of discouragement, God wants to convert us to hope.

- There is a vast difference between inspection and introspection. Morbid introspection is lethal. Inspection, on the other hand, is healthy and freeing.

- In order for inspection to occur, we must look away at something objective outside of ourselves, in order to accurately see ourselves.

- Always give preference to the spirit of contrition.

- When brokenness comes, time stands still. Forget the clock.

- Christ is our Sanctifier.

Mentoring Group Discussion

1. Why was discouragement so unthinkable to Armin?
2. What does encouragement have to do with the Holy Spirit?
3. What were the two R's Armin gave to deal with discouragement?
4. In your own words, describe the difference between inspection and introspection.
5. What does it mean in a practical way to be converted to hope?

Epilogue

Finishing Strong

I am of another generation, but for nearly thirty years I knew of the life of Armin Gesswein. As a New Yorker, I was familiar with this pastor and itinerant who made noises about revival and the necessity of prayer. As a child of immigrant Norwegians who christened me a Lutheran, I was fascinated about the stories of revival in Norway, stories attributed to Armin. But it was not until God changed me to recognize the critical role of prayer and revival in history that Armin's life and testimony came into focus. His passion for God (formed in the bosom of powerful manifestations of the Holy Spirit's grace), his stories of transformed people, churches and communities, his instruction in ministry, and, most of all, the days of prayer he led, helped frame in my soul the definition of a leader who seeks after God, moreover, a leader who runs his race joyfully and finishes well. Such is one who has fixed his eyes on Jesus, the Author and Perfecter of his faith. With many, many people I can testify: Armin, a friend and teacher, left a piece of himself affixed to my soul.

—Robert Bakke, Director,
National Prayer Accord,
Evangelical Free Church

For Rocky Balboa, finishing strong was pictured with his fists clenched over his head, standing center ring over his unconscious opponent stretched

157

out on the mat. For Eric Liddell in *Chariots of Fire*, it was breaking the tape in the quarter mile. Let me paint a picture for you of Armin Gesswein finishing strong. In fact, if I were to chisel a granite statute of Armin, this would be the pose.

The place is Nyack College, just north of New York City, overlooking the Tappan Zee Bridge. Armin is kneeling on a marble floor, a posture he maintained for nearly three hours. He is surrounded by a roomful of college and graduate school students, pastors and Christian leaders who are sprawled out in every imaginable direction.

Some are sleeping. Some are lying face down, others draped over each other. Many are fidgeting, trying desperately to find a comfortable position. Armin, on the other hand, is strong, vibrant, fresh. I vividly remember one of my college student buddies tapping me on the shoulder, with a gleam in his eye and with a wave of his hand, whispering, "Take a look at Armin." The contrast between the weary students and the robust Armin was a picture forever etched in my brain.

If you have ever looked on the face of someone who has been praying for a long time, you are likely to see a wrinkled forehead, puckered lips, frowning eyes and a generally sour look on their face. But Armin's countenance was the exact opposite! His eyelids were closed, but they seemed to glow with anticipation. His mouth was softly smiling as though he was savoring the moment. His cheeks and forehead were tight with anticipation, yet at the same time peaceful. His clasped hands were extended forward and high, almost equal in elevation to his face, which was tilted up as if looking off into the distance, expecting Someone important to walk into the room. And he had that expectation.

Take a look at Armin. Take a look at his countenance, his posture, his anticipation, his expectation. Take a look at his

longevity, his tenacity, his virility and nobility. Take a look at
his character.

Take a look at Armin. Look at his strength, his courage,
his endurance. Look at his youthfulness.

Take a look at Armin. As I looked at him surrounded by
wilting students, I immediately thought of the words: "Even
youths grow tired and weary, and young men stumble and
fall; but those who hope in [wait upon] the LORD will renew
their strength" (Isaiah 40:30-31). Though Armin was not
speaking, I could hear his voice commenting on these
words, saying, "That's what God wants us to be: three-speed
saints. They mount up with wings and fly. They run without
getting winded. And they walk without growing faint."

Armin was a three-speed saint, right up until the last conscious moments of his life, when in April 2001, long before
sunrise, he awoke in his mobile home for morning prayer. He
walked into his prayer room where, sometime later, he suf-
fered a massive stroke. Within the next forty-eight hours he
was in the glorious presence of the One who lives to make intercession for us.

As I sat squished like a sardine in the front row of his memorial service, I realized that while Armin had been a pastor, missionary, evangelist, revivalist, preacher, teacher,
prayer leader and Christian statesman, when all was said
and done, he was first and foremost the consummate
networker and mentor. Part of the reason he finished strong
was because of his well-connectedness, a feature of his ministry which, not surprisingly, was the outgrowth of corporate prayer. Armin explains it this way:

> In August of 1940 I came West for the first time. The
> only man I knew was Rev. Frank Sutherland, who had
> been part of our Long Island minister's prayer fellow-

ship. "Frank," I said, "let's phone two other ministers and ask if they would meet with us on Monday morning to pray for revival in their lives and churches." It worked. All four of us would be there: Frank Sutherland, Christian and Missionary Alliance pastor; Paul Sawtell, nondenominational pastor; Dale Satterthwait, Baptist pastor; and I, an ordained Lutheran. Our prayer time was strong. We agreed to meet again next Monday morning. We invited others, and a work of God began which has never stopped. To God be the glory!

Rev. William P. Nicholson, the famous Irish evangelist who was among the many who came to pray, called them the Monday Morning Men. They came from many backgrounds and denominations and from quite a distance. Rev. Herb Richardson, pastor of North Redondo Chapel, came faithfully every Monday by streetcar. "As we prayed together," Armin wrote, "we learned the secret of genuine one-accord Christian unity, the key to the book of Acts. True ecumenicity. Our unity was in Christ—deeper than our differences which could divide.

"We never had a fight or even a fuss—only love," he testified. "And the Holy Spirit was at work with His holy presence and power."

Along with weekly gatherings, they later developed a larger and somewhat longer monthly meeting, in which many more came. The spirit of prayer and revival moved them deeply.

In 1948 they took a third step and began a revival conference at Pacific Palisades which included lay leaders as well as pastors. They met twice a year and as many as 700 came. Prayer had priority and became the generator; times of refreshing came from the presence of the Lord. Revival blessings were reported as people received a new touch, and some a full transformation, in those conferences.

Ministers' prayer fellowships and revival conferences began to be held in other places: San Diego, Bakersfield, Fresno and Sacramento. Dr. Robert Munger was part of the early Los Angeles meetings when he became the minister of the First Presbyterian Church of Berkeley. He teamed up with Rev. Harold Erickson of the First Covenant Church of Oakland to lead many of our conferences at Mt. Hermon. Rev. William Dunlap developed prayer fellowships of ministers and revival conferences in the Chicago area. Rev. Allen Brown led some in Iowa, in Des Moines and at William Penn College (now William Penn University).

Billy Graham came to the conference at Pacific Palisades in 1949 and the spirit of prayer was strongly at work in our whole area. The heavens opened over his tent meetings and over his ministry, from which God launched his worldwide prayer ministry. Dr. J. Edwin Orr was very close to this work and was greatly used in these conferences. World Vision, Far East Broadcasting, World Opportunities and others looked to Gesswein for leadership. These remarkable leaders learned true fellowship with one another; they learned to bear one another's burdens, to help one another and to boldly obey what God was leading them to do. Together they found fellowship in revival-prayer.

The College of Prayer

When Christ went to heaven, He left behind an Upper Room prayer meeting. When Armin went to heaven, he similarly left behind the College of Prayer. In fact, he often affectionately referred to the College of Prayer as an Upper Room. It was his consummate effort of mentoring revival-prayer.

Armin's vision was to mentor Christian leaders to reach a lost world through a revived Church. He desired to establish a life-on-life, mentoring, training and equipping center where pastors and Christian leaders could come together privately for equipping and then go back to their ministry assignments and put it into practice.

In 1996 the first College of Prayer campus was started in metro Atlanta under the parent organization called "The Revival-Prayer Institute." Pastors from all over North America registered for the nine-module revival-prayer discipleship. At each module students enjoy three and a half days of instruction, intercession and interaction together.

The fall module emphasizes "Fullness," or the personal revival of the inner life by the Holy Spirit. The winter module emphasizes "Fulfillment," or the overflow and community impact of the revived life and revived church. The Fulfillment module covers such topics as prayer evangelism, prayer walking, prayer mapping, prayer journeys, neighborhood lighthouses of prayer, etc. The spring module emphasizes a particular prayer focus, such as deliverance, ministry, intercession training, or "keeping the home fires burning" (raising children who have a passion for Jesus).

Presenters at various modules have included David Bryant, Evelyn Christenson, Henry Blackaby, Wesley Duewel and others. In addition to metro Atlanta, we now have College of Prayer campuses in Beulah Beach, Ohio, and Calgary, Alberta, Canada. This next year we anticipate new campuses being established in Orlando, Florida; Philadelphia, Pennsylvania; and several new sites in Canada. The College of Prayer has been useful in bringing spiritual renewal to hundreds of pastors, pastors' wives and other Christian leaders. Already dozens of pastors have told us they would not be in the ministry today if not for the College of Prayer (COP). We are receiving invitations to plant COP campuses in Norway, Côte d'Ivoire and Hong Kong/China. Armin Gesswein's vision is being fulfilled.

The spiritual vitality nurtured at College of Prayer campuses is evidence of a legitimate work of God's Holy Spirit in our generation. Pastors and their people are tired of "playing church." They don't want to be fed "gospel-lite" any longer; they want the real deal. Rather than running all over the country to attend the latest church-growth seminar and bring back the notebook to put on their shelf next to last year's notebook, they want substance. They want authentic spiritual life. As Christ taught His early followers, He is teaching many of us that the spiritual reality we long for is found not in a conference but at the throne.

The College of Prayer is similar to a prayer summit in that it enjoys extended time of uninterrupted prayer, worship, repentance, cleansing, listening and renewal. But they are dissimilar in that the College of Prayer offers instruction and continuity. Essentially the same people return to each module, which leads to a deeper impact on one's life through extended accountability. It is not surprising that we have on file more than a dozen letters from grateful pastors who tell us that they would have dropped out of the ministry if not for the healing, freeing and refreshing impact of the College of Prayer. This grass roots, easily transferable, cost-efficient model could well become a paradigm God will use until Christ returns. (For more information see the web site www.collegeofprayer.org.)

Take a look at Armin. That's a picture that may never be chiseled in granite. It is, however, chiseled in my mind and in my heart. It is worth chiseling in yours as well.

Take a look at Armin. He was a rare man with a rare spirit. When God made him, He certainly tossed away the mold. The principles of revival-prayer, however, are eternal. And they are certainly worth a second look.

Take a look at Armin. Feast your eyes. Enlarge your soul. Catch a vision.

Take a look at Armin. Look at his lifestyle and passion. Look at his vision and his influence. Look at the fruit and look at the fulfillment.

Take a good, long, hard, lasting look at Armin. Drape your life over his for a while. Let him take you to school, the way he took many of us. Follow him as he followed Christ.

Summary

- Armin's countenance in prayer reflected his sense of anticipation and expectation.

- Three-speed saints mount up with wings and fly; they run without getting winded; they walk without fainting.

- Armin finished well at least partially because he was so well connected.

- True ecumenicity is a God-thing.

- The College of Prayer is an effort to take deeper the modern prayer movement so that it is not a mile wide and an inch deep.

Endnotes

Introduction—My Mentor, My Friend

1. Sherwood Wirt, "The Lost Prayer Meeting," *Decision*, March 1973, n.p.
2. Keith Anderson and Randy Reese, *Spiritual Mentoring* (Colorado Springs, CO: InterVarsity, 1999), p. 12.

Chapter 1—Prayer and the Upper Room

1. R.C.H. Lenski, *The Acts of the Apostles* (Minneapolis, MN: Augsburg, 1961), p. 39.
2. Jim Cymbala, *Fresh Wind, Fresh Fire* (Nashville, TN: Zondervan, 2000), pp. 50-51.

Chapter 2—Prayer and the Man Himself

1. George Mueller, as quoted by Armin Gesswein.

Chapter 3—Prayer and Jesus' Teaching

1. Armin Gesswein, *Sun Post News*, Friday, March 13, 1998.
2. Henry Blackaby, *Experiencing God* (Sunday School Board of SBC, 1990).

Chapter 4—Prayer and Jesus' Example

1. This concept is the essence of Armin's graduate school dissertation, "The Law of Revival." See Chapter 8 for a fuller explanation. Suffice it to say now that the reason our society continues to drift so dramatically toward increased immorality and corruption, yet continues to experience an absence of conviction, is because the Church is not receiving the fullness of the Holy Spirit to the measure Christ intends.

Chapter 6—Praying the Promises of God

1. Albert Barnes, *Barnes' Notes on Acts*.
2. Armin Gesswein, *Decision*, January 1988, n.p.

Chapter 7—Prayer and the Holy Spirit

1. Armin Gesswein, *How Can I Be Filled with the Holy Spirit?* (Camp Hill, PA: Christian Publications, 1999), pp. xi-xii.

Chapter 9—Prayer and the Sovereignty of God

1. Richard Loveless, *Dynamics of Spiritual Life: An Evangelical Theology of Renewal* (Downer's Grove, IL: InterVarsity Press, 1979), n.p.
2. Albert Barnes, *Notes on the New Testament*.
3. Ibid.